Institutions and the Economy

D0873518

Economy and Society

Institutions and the Economy

Francesco Duina

polity

Copyright © Francesco Duina 2011

The right of Francesco Duina to be identified as Author of this Work has been asserted in accordance with the UK Copyright, Designs and Patents Act 1988.

First published in 2011 by Polity Press

Polity Press
65 Bridge Street
Cambridge CB2 1UR, UK

Polity Press
350 Main Street
Malden, MA 02148, USA

All rights reserved. Except for the quotation of short passages for the purpose of criticism and review, no part of this publication may be reproduced, stored in a retrieval system, or transmitted, in any form or by any means, electronic, mechanical, photocopying, recording or otherwise, without the prior permission of the publisher.

ISBN-13: 978-0-7456-4829-3
ISBN-13: 978-0-7456-4830-9(pb)

A catalogue record for this book is available from the British Library.

Typeset in 11 on 13 pt Sabon
by Servis Filmsetting Ltd, Stockport, Cheshire
Printed and bound in Great Britain by MPG Books Group Limited, Bodmin, Cornwall

The publisher has used its best endeavours to ensure that the URLs for external websites referred to in this book are correct and active at the time of going to press. However, the publisher has no responsibility for the websites and can make no guarantee that a site will remain live or that the content is or will remain appropriate.

Every effort has been made to trace all copyright holders, but if any have been inadvertently overlooked the publisher will be pleased to include any necessary credits in any subsequent reprint or edition.

For further information on Polity, visit our website: www.politybooks.com

Contents

Figures and Tables

Figures

Tables

Abbreviations

Acquired Rights Directive (ARD)
Collective Redundancies Directive (CRD)
Coordinated Market Economies (CMEs)
European Union (EU)
Foreign Direct Investment (FDI)
Gross Domestic Product (GDP)
Incremental Product Innovation (IPI)
International Accounting Standards Board (IASB)
International Bank for Reconstruction and Development
    (IBRD)
International Development Association (IDA)
International Electrotechnical Commission (IEC)
International Financial Reporting Standards (IFRS)
International Monetary Fund (IMF)
International Non-Governmental Organizations
    (INGOs)
International Standards Organization (ISO)
Liberal Market Economies (LMEs)
New Institutional Economics (NIE)
North American Free Trade Agreement (NAFTA)
Radical Product Innovation (RPI)
Regional Trade Agreements (RTAs)
State-Owned Enterprises (SOEs)
Standard Operating Procedures (SOPs)
Standardization Organizations (SOs)

Abbreviations

Structural Adjustment Programs (SAPs)
US News and World Report (USNWR)
World Trade Organization (WTO)

Acknowledgments

While a doctoral student in sociology at Harvard University in the early 1990s, I took a seminar on institutionalist theory with John Campbell, now at Dartmouth College. The seminar changed my sociological understanding of the economy and of society more generally. When I joined the faculty at Bates College in 2000, I began offering a course in economic sociology with a heavy institutionalist perspective. My appreciation for institutionalist theory evolved during those years of intense interactions with some of the most intellectually dynamic and driven students one could ever have. This book owes much to Professor Campbell and those students.

Since 2004, I have had the honor of being a Visiting Professor at the Department of Business and Politics at the Copenhagen Business School. Founded by Ove Kaj Pedersen, the department is at the cutting edge of institutionalist research on national economic performance and the functioning of the international economy. I have benefited greatly from its many workshops, seminars, and research projects – and chapter 4 in particular draws heavily from my experience at the department.

Emma Longstaff at Polity Press approached me in 2008 to discuss her vision for a new series in economic sociology. She correctly saw the need for a number of texts that would order and clarify – for students but also scholars – most of the key concepts of this relatively new and growing discipline. I found the idea very exciting and told her that a book on institutions and the economy was sorely missing. Our conversations laid the groundwork for this project. Her guidance, along with that of Jonathan Skerrett at the press, helped me greatly in the planning and writing phases. The suggestions of three anonymous reviewers, in turn, proved incredibly useful for defining both the overall conceptual scope of the book and the specific topics it should cover.

I received funding from Bates College for research and travel support. This made it possible for two extraordinary undergraduates – Jared Bok and Ada Tadmor – to help me think through and write several sections of the book. Their diligent editorial support also proved invaluable. I am thankful to both for their positive mindset and work.

As always, I would then like to thank my wife, Angela, and children, Gianluca and Sofia, for their understanding and flexibility. Writing a book takes both time and energy. In a world where almost everything is finite, this means that I sometimes could not be with them when I should have. I am appreciative of their unconditional love and support.

Part I

Introduction

1

Institutions and the Economy

Institutions are everywhere. They affect how we eat, talk, conduct ourselves in public or in private, earn a college degree, play sports, and get married. They are both inside and outside of organizations – such as schools, hospitals, state administrative units, and baseball teams. Entire industries are rich with institutions, while international bodies such as the World Bank and the United Nations could not function without them. The objective of this book is to understand how institutions enable and shape a particular dimension of social life: the economy.

We should begin, then, by defining institutions. Alternative definitions abound, as we shall see in a few pages. This is not surprising: scholars from different intellectual traditions (from rational choice theory to neo-institutionalism, structuralism, phenomenology, and constructivism) and academic disciplines (economics, political science, and sociology above all) have over time sought to understand the nature of institutions and their impact on various aspects of social life. In this book, we adopt a definition of institutions embraced, fully or in part, by most economic sociologists.

Institutions are the formal and informal rules and practices that surround us as we go about our daily lives. At the formal level, they include public and private law (e.g., taxation and inheritance laws), standard operating procedures (SOPs) (e.g., written guidelines for how medical staff in emergency rooms should respond to patients seeking urgent attention), and the principles

3

ordering structures in governments, firms, and various types of associations (e.g., corporate statements defining the responsibilities and missions of different departments, such as marketing or accounting). At the informal level, they include traditions (e.g., families buying and then carving pumpkins for Halloween), routines (e.g., the steps that the International Bar Association takes to distribute information to its member lawyers worldwide), norms (e.g., the expectation held by many in Scandinavian countries that health-care provision should be universal), and shared but tacit assumptions about the functioning of the world (e.g., the widely held belief among staff at the World Bank that capitalism is the best type of economic system).

Institutions, then, are neither tangible nor visible. They affect how individuals, organizations, national governments, and even international entities operate, but are not the same thing as those actors. We may say that institutions have a life of their own, but also that their existence is intimately dependent on other aspects of society. The specific rules that set salary caps for professional basketball teams in the United States reflect, for example, the interests of players and team owners, the ability of these stakeholders to organize and voice their viewpoints, and the desire of fans and media venues alike to watch evenly balanced teams play. We may also say that institutions can vary greatly from each other. A handshake is as much an institution as the policies governing minimum balances in personal checking accounts at banks or the certifications found on packages of organically grown foods.

This book investigates the impact of institutions on the economy. What do we mean, then, by "the economy"? Individuals, organizations, nations, groups of nations, and international actors all engage in economic activity. Individuals buy and sell things all the time – food, clothes, cars, phones, tickets to concerts or sports events, and much more. A great number and variety of organizations produce services and products for the marketplace, and set up themselves internally to achieve their ends. Countries have and support entire industries. Often, they also join together to create transnational marketplaces. At a more global level, international actors – such as the World Bank or the United Nations

– provide funds, training, infrastructure, and other resources for economic development. All of this makes it difficult to generate a simple definition of the economy. As is the case for institutions, multiple definitions abound (Backhouse and Medema 2009). Most of those definitions, however, are not necessarily in contradiction or in tension with each other. For our purposes, then, an economy is a space where two or more actors enter into exchanges aimed at the improvement of the material or psychological well-being of one, some, or a large number of actors. This definition is either consistent with, or at least does not challenge, the majority of available views of what economic activity is about (see, for instance, Polanyi 1944: 31–2; Friedman 1980; Epping 2001: 3; and Wheelan 2002).

We will examine how institutions enable and shape economic life in society. The emphasis will be on "enable" and "shape." In some academic disciplines – neoclassical economics in particular – researchers have traditionally conceived of institutions as limiting economic life, as presenting obstacles to its ideal or proper functioning. We can call this a "negative" understanding of institutions. Imposing taxes on sales, for instance, is seen as discouraging people from producing and trading goods since a third party – the state, the city government, or whoever is imposing the tax – is depriving those involved in the exchange of some benefits. In line with the perspective of most economic sociologists, we will subscribe to a more "positive" interpretation of institutions. "Enable" means that institutions make much of economic life possible in the first place. Without institutions, the economy simply could not function. Investments in new product lines or in new production facilities, for instance, require that there be an enforceable and stable legal system. This is not to say that institutions are the only necessary prerequisite for economic activity. Other factors matter a great deal too. Some, like trust, are closely related to institutions (you would trust a surgeon to operate on your leg, for instance, because you know that she has undergone standard training, acquired diplomas, and so on). Others are less related to institutions (for example, the presence of good roads and railways).

Yet institutions do more than enable economic activity to take place. They also mold and even define – "shape" in the language of this book – in profound ways the very essence of that activity. Consider, for instance, the services offered by corporate accountants. Among those accountants, it is standard practice to think of corporations as having customers, suppliers, product-lines, and so on. It is also standard practice to assume that corporations are in a constant state of flux – that their profits after taxes vary, for example, from quarter to quarter. Corporate accountants are trained to think in these terms in business schools and in professional training programs. The federal tax code requires them to adopt this perspective. Business executives, understanding all this, hire those accountants for their services. The exchange of money for accounting services thus reflects these shared perspectives and practices, the business school programs that teach them, and the tax code that enforces them – all of which are institutions. We may even say that those institutions are at the heart of the exchange.

Throughout this book, we will stress something of major importance about how, exactly, institutions enable and shape economic life: the positive contribution of institutions has little to do with efficiency – that is, with decreasing costs, efforts, or the resources required for attaining something. We might be tempted to think that, if institutions help the economy operate, they must do so by making things more efficient. This has been the position of some economists since the 1970s. In fact, consistent with our sociological stance, our analysis will show something quite different. Institutions enable and shape economic life by making some things legitimate and others not, filtering and channeling in particular ways information and data, determining the formation and articulation of preferences, making and limiting options, generating an environment that is stable over time, defining the very essence of what is available in the marketplace, and much more. Briefly put, institutions provide the foundations and supporting structures for economic life.

Thus, we will also emphasize that it is practically impossible to think of economic life as something separate from its social context (Swedberg and Granovetter 2001: 8). This will be a profound realization – one that challenges the most basic assumptions of the modern discipline of economics and one that, once grasped, has both conceptual and practical implications. First, we will be able to explain economic phenomena more fully. We will have a deeper understanding, for instance, of why some products exist in the marketplace and others do not, consumers prefer some products to others, or some countries produce more environmentally sound products than others. Thus, second, we will be in a better position to suggest ways in which certain undesirable economic outcomes may be avoided and better ones be secured. Institutions, after all, are seldom fixed and are quite often the object, and partly the result, of contention and power dynamics. Think, for example, of the policies that determine what types of snacks and drinks are available in public schools (and thus what children are likely to eat and drink), or the formal and informal principles that drive budget negotiations within national governments or how international development agencies such as the International Monetary Fund (IMF) decide to spend their funds. None of these is fixed and all can in principle be changed.

We will carry out our analysis in four steps. We will move from the very micro (individual transactions) to the most macro (the global marketplace) dimensions of the economy as follows:

- Chapter 2: institutions and the economic behavior of *individuals*.
- Chapter 3: institutions and the economic behavior of *organizations*.
- Chapter 4: institutions and the economies of *nation-states*.
- Chapter 5: institutions and the *international economy*.

Chapter 2 will focus on the economic behavior of individuals. Most of us buy or sell something nearly every day of our lives. This happens in countless places, such as grocery stores, gas stations, movie theaters, and cyberspace. Institutions impact those transactions. Imagine yourself, for instance, at one of The Gap stores buying a shirt. What is the order of events? When, exactly, does the shirt become yours and stop belonging to the store? What rights does ownership give you? The transaction would not be possible without the existence of recognized property rights and agreed-upon procedures for how exchanges should unfold – two very important sorts of institutions. We will discuss the many ways in which a number of institutions enable and shape individual-level transactions.

In chapter 3, we will turn to organizations. These include firms, industry associations (e.g., employer associations, labor unions), interest groups (e.g., women's organizations, the American Association of Retired Persons), educational establishments (e.g., colleges, secondary public schools), hospitals, and more. The economic behavior of organizations refers to those actions and processes that organizations undertake or follow in order to acquire, manage, and distribute resources. We will try and understand that behavior. Why, for instance, do most business organizations have separate marketing, human resources, and accounting units? Most have CEOs, VPs, and secretaries. Where does this organizational design come from? What prompts organizations to conform to such a design? We will see, among other things, that organizations borrow from their environment blueprints that specify what legitimate organizations ought to look like. Those blueprints, which are institutions in their own right, seldom improve organizational efficiency or performance. But, by ensuring conformity with expectations, they give organizations access to valuable resources in society.

Chapter 4 will examine the impact of institutions on national economies. Countries like the United States or France are gigantic marketplaces. Therein, hundreds of industries (in sectors such as manufacturing, financial services, agriculture, etc.) employ millions of people. We will consider the performance of those economies and industries. We will ask why some countries perform better than others (Denmark, for instance, compared to India), and why countries specialize in certain industries and not others. We will then turn to the question of long-term transitions, and especially why countries experience major, protracted deteriorations or improvements in their economies (consider the successful trajectory of South Korea as opposed to the painful contraction of the

Zimbabwean economy), and how former communist and social-ist countries have migrated toward market capitalism. We will discuss the role of regulation, industrial relations, government structures and practices, and modes of interest representation. We will then examine how national economies have reacted to increased participation in the international economy. The global trade of goods and services, for instance, has put enormous pressures on labor markets, state-owned enterprises (SOEs), and trade barriers and tariffs. What role have national institutions played in mediating those pressures?

Economies are increasingly integrated at the transnational level. Chapter 5 will investigate the making and functioning of the international economy. Powerful international organizations such as the IMF and the World Bank try to stabilize and bolster the global marketplace. What sorts of rules and practices have those organizations promulgated? How have they sought to structure the international economy? Moreover, how do those organizations operate internally? How are policies formulated, interests represented, agreements reached? Further, the international economy is not necessarily global in nature. Regional trade agreements (RTAs) have mushroomed all over the world since the 1980s, with the aim of improving their member-states' competitiveness and productivity. RTA officials have used institutions (laws especially) to create those markets. What do those institutions look like, and why? What impact have they had on economic integration? Finally, international associations – such as the International Accounting Standards Board (IASB) – try and advance the interests of a great number of businesses, interest groups, and lobbies. What have their institutional initiatives been? And what impact have those had on the international economy?

As we make our way through the chapters, we will learn a great deal about how institutions enable and shape economic life. But we will also see that certain aspects of that relationship are far from being fully understood. Culture (values, belief systems, etc.), for instance, is rarely mentioned in institutionalist analyses of the economy; however, upon closer look, culture quite often figures in those accounts. For example, when we consider the rules that individuals and organizations must follow when engaging in economic activity (e.g., food producers are required to label their food with nutritional information), we see that they almost always reflect or incorporate widespread beliefs (such as that consumers have a right to know what they are about to eat or drink). Should we say more, then, about culture as we theorize about institutions and the economy? Is culture always a part of institutions? What is the difference between culture and institutions? Similarly, when it comes to institutional change, we still only have a basic understanding of how institutions evolve over time, especially when we consider institutions that operate at the international level – for instance, the rules agreed to by the representatives of the leading economies of the world on safe banking practices. What causes international institutions to change? And how does such change affect the international economy, national institutional factors, and national economic life? We will revisit these and other related questions in the concluding chapter of the book.

Before proceeding in our investigation, we would do well to spend some time clarifying a few basic ideas. First, until the twentieth century, few researchers took the role of institutions, however defined, in the economy seriously. Economists were the first to develop a sustained research agenda on the topic, with political scientists following thereafter. It was not until the 1990s that sociologists engaged in a serious investigation of the impact of institutions on economic life. What role did institutions play in the economy according to the first researchers? How did their accounts differ from later researchers? Why are these differences important? Section A below tackles these questions.

Second, there exist multiple and sometimes conflicting definitions of institutions. In this book, we have adopted a very specific definition – one that is in line with the perspective of most economic sociologists. We should be aware of the most important alternative definitions and think about the implications of choosing one definition over the others. What do we leave out from our analysis by subscribing to the view that institutions are the formal and informal rules and practices that surround us as we go about our daily lives? How does that perspective channel our discussion? We consider these matters in section B of this chapter.

Finally, we should be clear about how the study of institutions and the economy "fits" into the larger research agenda of economic sociology. Economic sociology is a relatively new and exciting field of research, and the task before us falls squarely into its mandate. Yet it is only one part of a larger project. Section C places this book in its larger disciplinary context.

A. The Study of Institutions in the Economy

Institutions have been around us since the birth of civilization. Interestingly, however, in the case of the economy at least, they did not become an explicit subject of investigation until the twentieth century. Before then, there were very few books or articles dedicated to the study of institutions, however defined, in the economy. Scholars did not specialize in that field and there were no college-level courses on the topic. Eventually, scholars from various social scientific disciplines began to turn their attention to institutions. Among the first were economists.

Economics

Some of the first researchers to claim that institutions, however defined, are important for the economy were economists. Between 1900 and the 1930s, John R. Commons and Thorstein Veblen, among others, put forth the basic tenets of "institutional economics" (Campbell 2004: 10). Their central, and in hindsight rather basic and rather sociological in spirit, insight was that economic transactions could not happen without supporting institutions. Laws, for instance, make private property possible and define how individuals interact with each other when buying and selling something (Commons 1931). Institutional economists offered some of the earliest, qualitative, and fairly non-theoretical explorations of institutions in the economy. By the 1950s and

1960s, however, their perspectives lost ground to a different school of thought – one much more focused on individual actors, the free market, and quantitative modeling of the economy (Swedberg and Granovetter 2001: 14–18).

The new approach took the label of neoclassical economics. Its proponents thought that interactions between buyers and sellers happen spontaneously, without any supporting mechanisms or structures. Buyers want certain things; sellers wish to sell certain things. Anything interfering with such simple dynamics can only distort the normal unfolding of events. No amount of top-down coordination or planning could improve matters. Instead, left to their own devices and in pursuit of their own selfish goals, individuals would not only pursue their objectives in the best possible fashion but also, in the aggregate, engage in self-adjusting dynamics. Prices would signal to producers how much to produce of something. Investments would be channeled in the most profitable industries. An "invisible hand," rather than governmental or other sorts of interventions, would guide the economy. A number of economists trained, or teaching, at the University of Chicago, such as Milton Friedman (1962) and George Stigler (1961; 1971), articulated these core principles of neoclassical economics especially well.

It took some time for economists to question the neoclassical paradigm. The first challenges came in the 1970s. Neoclassical economists simply assumed that information is abundant. This, however, is seldom the case. Buyers and sellers can easily fail to "meet" or find each other in the marketplace due to poor or distorted information. For instance, a person living in the northern suburbs of Chicago interested in purchasing a used Toyota Camry in great condition, low mileage, and for about $15,000 may never know that another person living 30 miles south of Chicago owns such a car and is eager to sell it for that price. Neoclassical economists did not, in turn, address the lack of predictability in the world and the fact that many investments and trades are, without supporting structures, inherently too risky to undertake. They also made questionable assumptions about the way certain public goods (such as clean air or a standing army) can ever come about.

Neoclassical economics seemed fraught with problems. What was it missing? How could it be rectified?

Attention turned to institutions. In the view of some economists, institutions can – and in fact already do every day – solve problems of poor information, risk, and uncertainty. Institutions can compensate for the inherent inefficiencies found in a pure marketplace. What was needed was a new theory for how the economy works. They called their new approach New Institutional Economics (NIE). NIE never displaced neoclassical economics from its position of dominance in the discipline, but it certainly had a major impact. The major works in NIE include Douglass North and Robert Paul Thomas's *The Rise of the Western World* (1973), Oliver Williamson's *Markets and Hierarchies* (1975) and *The Economic Institutions of Capitalism* (1985), Andrew Schotter's *The Economic Theory of Social Institutions* (1981), and Kenneth Arrow's *The Limits of Organization* (1974).

Each work took a particular perspective and focused on specific sorts of institutions. North and Thomas, for instance, tackled the question of uncertainty. Most individuals wish to be wealthy, of course. But as long as high degrees of risk surround them, they are unwilling to invest in the most promising enterprises and activities. What can solve this problem? What have societies put into place to reduce uncertainty? For North and Thomas, the answer was property rights. If individuals are guaranteed ownership of things (both present and future) in a regulated and predictable way, then they will engage in productive economic activity: "efficient organization entails the establishment of institutional arrangements and property rights that create an incentive to channel individual economic effort into activities that bring positive returns to them" (North and Thomas 1973: 1). It is not always easy to have recognizable and enforceable property rights in place, of course. Western countries managed to have them in place early on – something that probably accounts for their great wealth relative to the rest of the world. But many countries in Asia, Africa, and the Americas have so far struggled.

Williamson, in turn, stressed that every potential transaction has serious inefficiencies built into it that may prevent it from taking place. Williamson pointed, in particular, to transaction "costs" – or the fact that every transaction, however it takes place, requires resources or at the very least the loss of something valuable (such as time, for instance). Those costs generate a sort of "friction" in economic exchanges – slowing them down and sometimes preventing them from taking place altogether. Buyers, for example, must identify and then select among many suppliers. This requires gathering information, evaluating, and comparing – all activities that cost something. Then agreements must be negotiated, drafted, and safeguarded (Williamson 1985: 20). Institutions – especially those found in firms and other organizations – offer some of the most effective ways of dealing with these costs. There, a variety of actors who might otherwise function in the marketplace (such as human resource specialists, managers, and laborers) are brought under the same roof and asked to enter into repeated, controlled, and generally exclusive exchanges. Policies and regulations guide their behavior. Bargaining over prices need not happen every time. Information is easily shared. And there is a reduced need for quality controls for each and every exchange.

We are already in a position to make a few key observations about NIE. Its proponents viewed institutions as servants of the interests of individual actors. Institutions are tools, conduits, and means. They are created to fulfill a function. They are subordinate to something else and do not enjoy an independent existence. In the words of Schotter, "economic and social systems evolve the way species do. To ensure their survival and growth, they must solve a whole set of problems that arise as the system evolves. Each problem creates the need for some adaptive feature, that is, a social institution." Thus, interestingly, the mission of "social scientists is to infer the evolutionary problem that must have existed for the institution as we see it to have developed" (Schotter 1981: 1–2). And, importantly, if societies do not manage to produce such institutions, they are bound to fail. Again, as Schotter put it, "those societies that create the proper set of social institutions survive and flourish; those that do not, falter and die" (Schotter 1981: 2).

Political science

Political scientists joined the institutional turn in the 1970s and 1980s (Peters 2005). The study of institutions was not new for them, of course. Since the times of ancient Greece, students of politics such as Aristotle and Plato had recognized that there exist different political systems (such as democracies and aristocracies). They also understood that different sorts of institutions operate within those systems. Consider, for instance, the rules dictating how issues are debated in a dictatorship versus an oligarchy. Throughout the following centuries, thinkers such as St Augustine, Thomas Aquinas, Thomas Hobbes, Montesquieu, and Jean-Jacques Rousseau expanded and refined those analyses. But these were matters of political theory or comparative politics above all. Driving the debates was a desire to find the best political system or, at the very least, to understand the differences between alternative systems. Thus, these thinkers seldom discussed the relationship between institutions and the economy.

Political scientists turned their attention to the economy after World War II. How does politics affect the economy? How does the economy, in turn, affect politics? As they pondered these questions, most thinkers in the 1950s and 1960s embraced two paradigms that had little to do with institutions: rational choice theory and behaviorism (Peters 2005: 12). Both perspectives placed individuals (and to a lesser extent groups of individuals) at the very center of policymaking processes, bargaining, international relations, and every other political phenomenon of consequence for economic activity. In the case of rational choice theory, this meant paying attention to how presumably rational actors (in politics or the economy) pursue their preferences so as to maximize the likelihood that those preferences are realized (or, as theorists put it, that their utility is maximized). Politicians, for instance, can be said to be preoccupied above all with their own re-elections. Given this, they are bound to pursue the economic policies most likely to help them achieve that goal (rather than those most likely to benefit society as a whole). This was the argument of Anthony Downs (1957), among others. In the case of behaviorism, it meant focusing on key socio-psychological characteristics of individuals – such as legislators – as key explanatory variables (Wahlke et al. 1962).

The turn to individuals was in effect an embrace of the world-view of neoclassical economists – especially when it came to rational choice theory and its assumptions of preferences and utility maximization. It was also a significant departure from the historical roots of the discipline. After all, for centuries, political philosophers – even if not concerned with the economy – had thought about systems, structures, and things bigger than individual actors. Rational choice theory remains to this date a major paradigm in the discipline. In an important and relatively recent book, for instance, Margaret Levi accounted for the fiscal policies of the state in terms of the self-interested objectives of the rulers. As she put it, "all the actors who compose the polity, including the policymakers, are rational and self-interested" (Levi 1988: 2–3). Given this, their aim will be to maximize revenues accruing to the state, for this will increase their powers and influence.

Yet it also did not take too long before a counter-revolution started to spread. Several scholars began to appreciate the fact that the contexts in which individuals operate matter a great deal. The immense power of politics over the economy could not be understood without reference to those contexts. The first works in this vein were published in the 1970s and 1980s. Among the most important was the work of Harvard political scientist Peter Hall (1986) and his analysis of economic policymaking in Great Britain, France, and the United States. Hall did not reject rationalist accounts of policymaking. What he stressed, however, was that the way in which those actors "related" (could access, pressure, etc.) to the state shaped in significant ways how much and what those actors could get out of the state. Indeed, it even shaped how actors came to define and articulate their own preferences. Because such relationships were fairly stable and set, Hall referred to them as institutions: "We must," he wrote, "move beyond the view of policy-making implicit in most economic texts ... there exists a certain institutional logic to the process of economic intervention in the industrialized democracies" (Hall 1986: 4 and 5).

That logic, he added, concerns how "formal rules, compliance procedures, and standard operating practices ... structure the relationship between individuals in various units of the polity and the economy" (Hall 1986: 19).

Hence, Hall saw that institutions had a life of their own. Others followed his path and in so doing became pivotal in the formation of a school of thought known as "historical institutionalism." Among the most influential contributors were Kathleen Thelen (1999) and Paul Pierson (2004). Their models were far less relational than Hall's. Instead, in their view, time is of central importance. For instance, policy choices made at Time 1 channel and limit choices made at Time 2. Formal and informal policy-making practices, in turn, are "self-reinforcing": they generate outputs, incentive structures, habits, and other factors which ensure that those actors follow those practices again later in time. Historical institutionalists thus observed a certain "path dependence" in the workings of institutions: there is almost always some continuity in institutional dynamics over time, and abrupt and drastic deviations are very rare. These insights could apply to a great variety of cases. Pierson, for instance, used them to understand the development of welfare policies in the United States as well as the European Union (EU)'s pursuit of economic integration. Steinmo (1993) applied them to fiscal policy in Sweden, the United Kingdom, and the United States.

Despite the rise of historical institutionalism, however, most political scientists to this day subscribe – much like exponents of NIE – to a rationalist interpretation of institutions in the economy. The paradigm has assumed the label of "rational choice institutionalism." Actors struggle to advance their interests and, as they do so, create institutions to facilitate the attainment of their objectives. Of course, different actors prefer different institutional arrangements. Compromises are reached, however, whereby particular arrangements benefit those involved not fully but more so than if such compromises had not been reached. We are in "Pareto-optimal" spaces – something that Hall himself has come to partially embrace – or situations in which outcomes are such that no one can be made better off without making someone else worse off. Thus, in a recent piece on institutions and capitalism, Hall and Thelen (2009: 7) proposed that "the persistence of institutions depends not only on their aggregate welfare effects but also on the distributive benefits that they provide to the underlying social or political coalitions; and not only on the Pareto-optimal quality of such equilibria but also on continuous processes of mobilization through which the actors test the limits of the existing institutions." In other words, institutions exist because they make life better for everyone in general but also benefit key groups in society. They also come regularly under pressure from various stakeholders, who seek to ensure that their utility continues to be maximized as time goes on (Hall and Thelen 2009: 10). Hence, consistent with the view held by economists, for most political scientists institutions are subservient and ultimately not an integral part of the economy.

Sociology

Sociologists came to the study of institutions and the economy perhaps somewhat later than political scientists and economists. This was certainly not due to a prolonged love affair with methodological individualism – or the belief that whatever happens in society can best be understood by paying attention to individuals above all. At the very core of the discipline is the insight that individuals act in a context – and that that context should be at the center of any analysis. Moreover, the founders of sociology – Marx, Weber, and Durkheim, in particular – certainly paid considerable attention to the institutional underpinnings of capitalism (Campbell 2004: 3). The late turn to institutions came primarily as a function of attention going to other variables, such as culture, politics, power asymmetries, class stratification and conflict, and structural inequalities at the national and international levels.

When they finally turned to the economy and institutions – primarily in the 1980s and 1990s – sociologists brought to the table a rather unique perspective. They made quite clear that the individual is secondary to the functioning of the economy. Institutions do not exist as reflections of, or tools for, the advancements of rational actors' selfish interests. They do not generate Pareto-optimal outcomes where no one can be made better off without making someone else worse off. Interests, utility maximization, purpose, and other such terms are taken out of the equation. Institutions impact the economy in an altogether different manner. They are the context in which economic life takes place: the economy is embedded in institutional arrangements (Granovetter 1985). Moreover, under the sociological view, institutions affect the formation of economic actors in the first instance – who they are, what they want, and how they go about pursuing their objectives. Institutions sometimes enable, sometimes undermine, and very often give economic life its particular shape. Given this, it is quite difficult to conceive of economic life as truly separate from its institutional environments. This is not to suggest that the economy and institutions are one and the same thing; rather, it is to underscore the intimate and complex relationship between the two (Brinton and Nee 1998).

This, of course, was in part the message of political scientists working in the historical institutionalist tradition. But working within that tradition, sociologists amplified and refined the message of historical institutionalism. Some did so by theorizing not necessarily on the economy as such but on all major dimensions of social life – including the state, social movements, revolutions, interest group representation, and more. The most important examples in this regard are the works of Theda Skocpol (1984; 1995), James Mahoney (2000), and Margaret Weir (1993). Many others, as we shall see throughout this book, did so by tackling very specific aspects of economic life, ranging from the level of individual actors all the way to transnational and global dynamics.

Sociologists added additional key insights when working within a third tradition of institutional analysis: "organizational institutionalism" (as opposed to rational choice or historical institutionalism). Organizations of all kinds – trade unions, firms, state offices, industry associations, international agencies, and so on – engage in economic behavior. How do those organizations structure themselves internally and operate, exactly, in order to achieve their objectives? Traditional accounts of organizational behavior assumed a high degree of rationality and efficiency: organizations look and act as they do (and change over time) in order to ensure the advancements of their constituents' goals or simply their own survival as entities (classical sociologists like Weber and Durkheim had written much on this last point). The new breed of organizational sociologists argued something quite different and rather revolutionary.

First, we must distinguish between the formal rules of an organization and what *really* happens on a daily basis. The two are often quite different from each other. In the language of Meyer and his colleagues, they often "decouple" over time (Meyer and Rowan 1977). Thus, for instance, though in principle in a given firm the vice president of manufacturing should work closely with the CEO to map out a strategy for the coming year, we observe that something quite different occurs: the most important consultations happen with the vice president of research and development. Decoupling happens because the official institutional setup of organizations often follows not principles of efficiency or rationality but, instead, "myths," or established and often outdated blueprints available in society for what things "ought" to look like. Accordingly, to achieve concrete objectives, people and units inside organizations develop separate and more effective routines (Westphal and Zajac 2001).

Second, and closely related to the first point, despite the existence of alternative and unofficial ways of operating, much of what happens in an organization is ultimately neither rational nor efficient. Decoupling itself causes inefficiencies. Organizations are in turn full of idiosyncratic fashions, habits, inertia, and symbols (Zucker 1986). Actors make sense of the world around them through established – but far less than effective – patterns of information recognition and processing (for instance, data on sales reaches sales and marketing officials in prepackaged formats that are not very meaningful or actionable; those officials therefore deconstruct and reorder that data for their own use). Moreover, organizations exist in environments with other similar organizations. Those environments generate pressures for conformity in certain rules and practices, again regardless of actual effectiveness (Strang and Still 2004). Organizations borrow from each other based on what *appear* to be successful models. There are "mimetic" forces at work. As such, organizational leaders follow what scholars call a "logic of appropriateness" rather than one of instrumentality (Powell and DiMaggio 1991). These proved to be powerful insights that shaped in multiple ways our understanding of organizations and their actions and processes, and of economic life more generally.

Clearly, then, the question of how institutions impact the economy is now part of the research agenda of several disciplines. Our concern in this book is primarily with the sociological perspective, though we will also discuss works by scholars in other disciplines – political scientists especially – if in line with that perspective. Most of the works considered will fall within the boundaries of historical and organizational institutionalism, a few will be in line with rational choice institutionalism, and several will simply defy simple theoretical classifications. We will not be too worried about theoretical inclinations. Our goal will be to discover and articulate, as clearly and concretely as possible, the sociological perspective on how institutions enable and shape economic life.

B. Defining Institutions

This book is about institutions and their impact on economic life. We opened this chapter with an explicit definition of institutions. It is important to understand how that definition fits within the realm of existing definitions. Numerous social scientists have of course offered various definitions. Indeed, there are entire essays written on the breadth and evolution of those definitions (Duffield 2007). This is both a result of particular disciplinary and personal perspectives but also the fact that there is more than one way to define something, as Aristotle (1999) noted well over 2,000 years ago in his *Metaphysics*. We could look at the function of something, for instance, or its appearance, substance, how it changes over time, or some other property. How, then, have scholars defined institutions? Perhaps the simplest way to survey the vast array of available definitions is to recognize that there exist two rather polar schools of thought about the constitution of institutions. For some scholars, institutions are very concrete, highly structured, and formal "things." For others, they are very amorphous, loosely (if at all) structured, and very informal "things." For many other scholars, institutions are something in between these two opposite ends of the spectrum. We can begin at one extreme. Before we do so, we should also note that virtually all scholars agree on at least two aspects of institutions: institutions are fairly stable entities (i.e., if they change at all, they typically do so slowly), and institutions exert some sort of influence on actors in society (Peters 2005: 18–19).

According to perhaps the most formal approach, institutions are tightly structured entities – such as parliaments, courts, trade unions, firms, and various sorts of associations – whose parts relate to each other in clearly and often officially prescribed ways. We can think of institutions as highly organized spaces. They stand in contrast to other spaces in society, such as networks of friends or the telecommunications industry. There, the relevant units (individuals, firms, etc.) relate to each other in a more fluid and less pre-established manner. Importantly, from this perspective, the rules specifying the relationship between units are not considered institutions. Institutions are the entire entities. This was the view of many scholars from the nineteenth and early twentieth centuries, such as Theodore Woolsey (1877) and Woodrow Wilson (1890) in his academic work. Many important contemporary scholars, such as Theda Skocpol (1985) and Lisa Martin (1993: 423), subscribe at least in part to this stance.

A more common approach among contemporary scholars is to think of institutions as the formal rules structuring the activities of single actors or units. Thus, parliaments and trade unions, for example, are not institutions. The official principles ordering the internal functioning of those entities are institutions. But we can also go beyond the internal operations of an entity and consider how it relates to other entities in its environment. There, too, we are likely to find formal rules. For instance, constitutional and administrative law in the United States specifies not only how Congress ought to operate internally but also how it should relate to the legislative or judiciary branches of government. Similarly, firms have by-laws that establish their managerial structure and the role and function of the board of directors, but also have principles that guide their interactions with the media or investors, for example. Any given country, in addition, will have a legal system that will expect firms to behave in certain ways in society.

A good example of this sort of definitional approach can be found in the work of Peter Hall. As he put it in his comparative analysis of economic policy in the United Kingdom, France, and the United States, "the concept of institutions is used here to refer to the formal rules, compliance procedures, and standard operating practices that structure the relationship between individuals in various units of the polity and the economy" (Hall 1986: 19). As he acknowledges, these institutions have both a "formal status" and a "relational character" (Hall 1986: 19). Several scholars of international institutions subscribe to this definition (Duffield 2007: 4–6). In the words of Simmons and Martin, for instance, "most scholars have come to regard international institutions as sets of rules meant to govern international behavior"; institutions are rules "that forbid, require, or permit particular kinds of actions" (Simmons and Martin 2002: 194).

Crucially, however, far less formal things can also be considered institutions. Unofficial practices, routines, and even habits are, according to many scholars, institutions. It may be difficult to identify them in any given setting. They are not spelled out in any legal text or contract, for example. Instead, they reflect something that exists primarily in people's minds and simply occurs in everyday life on a regular basis. But their abstract qualities do not undermine their existence in any way. As is the case for their more formal counterparts, they affect both what happens at the individual and organizational levels, or in society as a whole (Powell and DiMaggio 1991; Finnemore 1996). Consider, for instance, those firms in which CEOs traditionally send out quarterly newsletters to their employees, or the way in which countries have learned to bargain with each other at the World Trade Organization

(WTO) over tariff barriers. Consider, as well, the way in which lobbying groups have learned to approach legislators. Do they send them policy papers? Do they provide them with data? Do they invite them to conferences and events? Guidebooks outlining how these things should take place in most cases do not exist. Yet these behaviors, if established and repeated over time, can be considered institutions. This "softer" approach to institutions has been dubbed at times "constructivist," sometimes "cognitive," sometimes something else altogether.

Economic sociologists – as is the case for most sociologists – have favored more "informal" definitions of institutions. But many have also subscribed to more "formal" definitions – though seldom have they embraced the early views of institutions as concrete organizations (such as parliaments). They have therefore produced rather hybrid definitions of institutions. For example, in Neil Fligstein's view, "institutions refer to shared rules, which can be laws or collective understandings, held in place by custom, explicit agreement, or tacit agreement" (Fligstein 1996: 658). And for John Campbell institutions "consist of formal and informal rules, monitoring and enforcement mechanisms, and systems of meaning that define the context within which individuals, corporations, labor unions, nation-states, and other organizations operate and interact with each other" (Campbell 2004: i).

For the purposes of this book, we will therefore adopt a fairly broad definition of institutions – one that is in line with the perspective of many economic sociologists (Morgan et al. 2010): institutions are the formal and informal rules and practices which impact the economic behavior of individuals and organizations, the economies of nation-states, and economic life at the international level. At the formal level, they include various types of law (administrative, constitutional, private, public, corporate, and so on), SOPs (codes of conduct and internally mandated guidelines, and the principles laying out the formal structures in governments and various types of organizations. At the informal level, they include traditions (for instance, the expectation that parents buy gifts for their children's birthdays or the fact that the typical workday begins at 9 a.m. and ends at 5 p.m.), routines (such as drinking one cup of coffee before going to work), and widely shared but tacit assumptions about the functioning of the world (for example, the belief that corporations generate something called profits which are then distributed among the shareholders). Our choice of definition has one major implication for the discussion in the following pages: we will not examine the impact of organizations on the economy. Organizations, according to our definitional stance, are greatly affected by, but are not, institutions.

C. *What Economic Sociologists Study (besides Institutions)*

The discipline of economic sociology is quite new. The founders of sociology certainly addressed the economy. But most sociologists did not really focus on it as a formal and distinct subject of enquiry until the 1980s, when Mark Granovetter (1985) published his work on the embeddedness of the economy in society. The Economic Sociology Section of the American Sociological Association was formed in 1990. The first introductory texts, such as those by Guillen et al. (2002), Smelser and Swedberg (2005), Dobbin (2004a), and Granovetter and Swedberg (2001), were published several years later. The same can be said of more specialized texts, such as those of Cetina and Preda (2004), DiMaggio (2001), and Fligstein (2001). It did not take long, however, for economic sociologists to specialize in rather diverse areas of inquiry. We cannot cover the span of their work in a few paragraphs. But we can discuss here the most important variables, besides institutions, which most researchers point to as explaining, driving, or simply shaping key aspects of the economy.

At the heart of some of the most interesting works is culture. In her seminal work on payments, for instance, Zelizer (1996a) showed how monetary exchanges are inevitably infused with subtle ideas about gift giving, entitlement, and compensation. In her work on children (Zelizer 1996b), she demonstrated that societies assign economic worth to children on the basis of ideas about family, responsibility, life, and death. In an intriguing analysis of fair trade and coffee consumption, Linton et al. (2004) in turn emphasized that fair trade coffee consumption is a profoundly symbolic act – one that asserts a person's beliefs about the world and justice. And in a study of egg and sperm donations, Almeling (2007) unveiled how recipients and industry professionals approach egg donors very differently from how they approach sperm donors. Relying on stereotypical beliefs about men and women, they come to see egg donors as being engaged in an altruistic act and sperm donors as being interested primarily in a business transaction.

All these scholars share a view of economic activity as being deeply affected by values, meaning structures, shared ideas about the world, and other elements of culture. At times, as we shall see in this book, institutions play a role in their accounts. For instance, international rules about coffee certification schemes shape the sort of meaning structures and values consumers develop when thinking about coffee (Linton et al. 2004), much like religious denominations affect people's ideas of work, savings, and proper ways of spending money (Keister 2008). Institutions, in other words, often shape culture in the first instance, though it can also be the case that culture shapes institutional factors that have an impact on economic behavior – as Aguilera and Jackson (2010) showed, for example, in their discussion of cultural settings across the world and their influence on corporations' governance rules and practices. In other instances, institutions simply do not appear to matter. In all cases, the point is one and the same: culture represents an important and independent variable that influences the unfolding of economic life in society.

A more structural approach concerns networks (Mizruchi et al. 2006). Buyers, sellers, firms, distributors, and other actors in the economy never function in isolation. They typically enjoy close relationships with a few other actors, and distant relationships with a larger number of actors. Those relationships determine a lot of what takes place in the marketplace. College graduates looking for a job, for instance, often rely on their family members and friends to find out who might be hiring, help them secure an interview, and guide them through negotiations once they receive an offer. Migrants depend on each other to access loans and other sources of capital (Portes and Sensenbrenner 1993). Many law firms depend on referrals for new client development and doctors routinely send patients to each other. At the level of entire industries, producers and suppliers interlock with each other at various levels, adapt their behaviors in light of what others have done (or will perhaps do), and constantly send each other valuable signals (explicit or not) (White 2002). Thus, as Carruthers and Babb observed, "people use their social networks to gather all kinds of information about job openings, new products, market opportunities, what the competition is up to, what their customers want, and so on. They even use networks to secure favors" (Carruthers and Babb 1999: 47).

If we move away from the open market and turn to the internal workings of organizations, we also see the powerful impact of networks. Employees know some of their colleagues better than others. In one firm, a manager may have extensive links to other managers; in another firm, managers may work in relative isolation. In colleges, some faculty members know the trustees very well, while other faculty members have never met them. These differences impact how economic decisions are made – where money is invested, what products and services are aggressively marketed, and so on.

On the whole, network theorists stress that networks can vary in size, duration, and strength. They also emphasize that different actors are positioned quite differently in networks: some have extensive and very rich networks, others only minor ones. Sociologists refer to these differences as variations in social capital (Lin et al. 2001; Fernandez et al. 2000). They point out, as well, that the impact of networks is at times mediated by other variables, including institutions. For instance, as Mizruchi et al. (2006) recently argued, networks have influenced the way large American corporations use debt, but decreasingly so due, in part, to the rise of professional experts (i.e., individuals who successfully undergo certification programs and training) in the finance industry, and the resulting spread of new expectations and procedures for borrowing.

The economy, in turn, could not function without trust. When we purchase a cappuccino at our favorite coffee shop, we simply assume that it comes with unspoiled milk and that, if we hand $10 to the person behind the register, we will get the correct change back. If we hop on a bus to go across town, we assume that the driver is knowledgeable about the route he is to follow. At times, institutions are put into place to enable us to learn more about the trustworthiness of other people. This has happened, for instance, on eBay with the voluntary scoring system that ranks both buyers and sellers (Kuwabara 2005). But in other cases we develop trust as a result of repeated interactions with others, on the basis of knowledge that in historical or in statistical terms the people around us have proven themselves to be reliable and honest. Trust, then, is something different from institutions and an important facilitator of economic life. Accordingly, it has been the subject of several important studies in economic sociology (Cook 2001; Abolafia 2001).

Additional variables influencing economic life include power (Fligstein 1990; Roy 1997), status (Benjamin and Podolny 1999), and groups of individuals and organizations with similar interests or needs (Keister 2000). These, too, sometimes exert clearly independent forces on the economy, while at times they interact with institutions. We could continue but need not, for we are now in a position to proceed with our investigation cognizant of the basic landscape of economic sociology. We will turn to the economic behavior of individuals first.

Part II

The Impact of Institutions

2

Individuals

Institutions enable and shape the economic behavior of individuals. Most of us buy or sell something every day of our lives. This happens in stores and other physical spaces, but also in virtual spaces, such as Expedia or eBay. We buy or sell countless things – from physical objects (an orange or a computer, for instance) to intangible services (such as life insurance or a college education). Economists tend to view our transactions as reflective of individual preferences: a person happens to want something that someone else wishes to sell. Sociologists do not necessarily believe that preferences are unimportant. They insist, however, that other factors play a major role in determining our behaviors, with institutions being among the most consequential ones.

Institutions influence all of the following:

A. The attributes and qualities of the items being bought and sold.
B. What is allowed and not allowed in the market.
C. What we know and do not know as we engage in the marketplace.
D. How we carry out our transactions.
E. Who the parties in the exchange are.
F. Why we wish to buy or sell something in the first place.

The impact of institutions is multifold, therefore. Institutions do more than facilitate or limit transactions: they also impact directly what those transactions are all about. We will discuss these ideas in detail in the coming pages as we consider, in order, points A through F. As we proceed, we will repeatedly run into a number of key concepts. For easy reference, table 2.1 identifies those concepts. In the next section, we turn to the objects we buy and sell in the marketplace.

Table 2.1   Key concepts for the economic behavior of individuals

Key concept	Definition
Product attributes	Physical and abstract qualities of a product
Market boundaries	Invisible barriers allowing certain products into the formal market and relegating others to the informal economy or non-existence
Information	Data we have about ourselves, others, products, and the world
Property rights	Authority over the use and consumption of something
Economic identity	Role an individual assumes when entering into economic exchanges
Preference formation	Process by which we develop a desire for something

A. Objects of Desire

The explosion of specialty coffee products in the United States in the 1990s was astounding. In the 1980s, very few Americans could be seen sipping cappuccinos or lattes at corner coffee shops or in their cars. Most people drank mediocre cups of coffee sold at very low prices. They did not discriminate much in terms of taste, aroma, or origins. Then came a revolution and in a matter of a few years millions of people added a new ritual to their daily routines. By 2008, according to the American Specialty Coffee Association, the market for specialty coffee had reached an astounding $14 billion – a sevenfold increase since the mid-1990s. Today, many people's mornings would not be complete without a stop at a

Starbucks or Seattle's Best Coffee shop, requesting a customized drink, and paying premium prices. For a few minutes, they can leave the world behind and walk into a sophisticated ambience – muted, pastel colors blended with trendy music, Italian and French-sounding words (such as Venti or Grande), wonderful aromas, and professional-looking people both behind the counters and among the clientele.

It is a soothing and rewarding experience during which customers can at once relax for a moment and find confirmation that they belong to a refined segment of the population. "We try to create, in our stores," stated Starbucks founder and CEO Howard Schultz, "an oasis, a little neighborhood spot where you can take a break, listen to some jazz, and ponder universal or even whimsical questions over a cup of coffee" (Schultz 1997: 12). In the beginning, it amounted to pure self-indulgence. Over time, however, it has evolved into something quite subtler. Customers now believe that their purchases can help others: "fair trade" coffee – priced a little higher, certainly, but so that faraway coffee farmers can live a respectable life and forests can be saved – is now available in most specialty outlets (Bacon et al. 2008). Mocha drinking thus comes with a moral dimension (Howley 2006). Here is what a Starbucks paper cup stated in late 2010:

> You. Bought 228 million pounds of responsibly grown, ethically traded coffee last year. Everything we do, you do. You stop by for a coffee. And just by doing that, you let Starbucks buy more coffee from farmers who are good to their workers, community and planet. Starbucks bought 65% of our coffee this way last year – 228 million pounds – and we're working with farmers to make it 100%. It's using our size for good, and you make it all possible. Way to go, you.

A symbol accompanied by this slogan also appears: "Shared Planet ™ – You and Starbucks. It's bigger than coffee."

Products, then, are very rich with attributes. Some are physical – such as the taste of coffee. But others are more abstract – such as the fact that the milk in the latte that we drink comes from cows which, instead of living with chains around their necks, can graze as nature intended on a farm's hills, or the fact that a farmer was paid more than industry average for picking coffee beans. All contribute to making the product into what it is. Though it may not be obvious at first, institutions play a very important role in shaping those attributes. Consider first the case of "certifications."

In the realm of food, a farmer growing corn cannot simply label her products "organic." The United States Department of Agriculture regulates production and standards through its National Organic Program and the Organic Foods Production Act – both institutions. Butter producers in France cannot simply call their products "Beurre des Deux-Sèvres." They must instead prove that their butters meet the requirements set out in the Appellation d'Origine Controllée program – another institution – just like grape growers in Peru must comply with the relevant regulations set out by the Consejo Regulador de la Denominacion de Origen in order to label their liquors "pisco." In the case of "fair trade" coffee, the certificates come from organizations such as TransFair and Max Havelaar, which have fought hard over the years to promote their ideas of justice and sustainability (Linton et al. 2004). If approved, certified products can be adorned with valuable stamps, symbols, acronyms, and the like.

Certifications have become an integral component of the agrifood business (Hatanaka and Busch 2008). But they apply to much more than food, of course. Banks advertise the fact that they are members of the Federal Deposit Insurance Corporation, colleges that they are accredited by agencies formally recognized by the United States Department of Education (such as the Northwest Commission on Colleges and Universities), and childcare providers that they are licensed by the local authorities to function. Certifications are issued by government bodies, but also by industry associations and other entities which have managed, invariably through power and other forms of political struggles, to assert themselves and their authority over time. Certifications do not necessarily amount to legal assertions. Yet, as formal practices following explicit sets of rules, they are institutions nonetheless.

What, exactly, do certifications add to a product? Much depends on the certification in question. Most, however, endow the product with a guarantee of quality or fairness. Typically granted by a third – and presumably independent – entity in light of pre-established standards, they render explicit something that otherwise would have been unclear. We, the consumers, thus gain a feeling of certainty, safety, and moral righteousness – regardless of the fact that, upon closer scrutiny, we may actually know rather little about the standards in question or the actual process of certification (Howley 2006).

Awards and recommendations given by industry associations, observers, and commentators for particular products obtain a similar effect. Auto magazines (e.g., *Motor Trend*) announce the best new cars of the year, while wine magazines publish their rankings of wines from different countries and regions. It also happens in the medical profession when the American Academy of Pediatricians, to name one association, recommends certain medicines or remedies for children's health conditions. The regularity and established history of those awards and recommendations make them institutions, and their association with specific products changes how the public perceives those products. The 2010 Subaru Outback, for example, won the prestigious Motor Trend "SUV of the Year" award. The award served as a major stamp of approval – and was naturally advertised by Subaru at every turn. It changed the image of the Outback, even though in practical terms nothing was different in the vehicle itself.

Awards, recommendations, and certifications, however, ultimately apply to a small percentage of products in the market. Much more common are the various regulations about safety, health, functionality, and appearance that apply to nearly all consumer products and services. Those regulations shape in profound ways the very essence of those products and services. For one thing, they define their core components. In the EU, for example, legislators have passed hundreds of laws specifying the key ingredients and characteristics of anything from fresh fish to the wipers of automobiles (Duina 2006). Toys, for instance, must comply with many, and very specific, chemical, mechanical, physical, and electrical requirements (Directive 88/378 of 1988). Anything that deviates from these specifications simply cannot be sold in the EU marketplace.

Yet, what is more, regulations can also shape the subtler qualities of products – such as their riskiness or sexiness. For instance, in the United States, individuals younger than twenty-one years of age cannot consume alcohol, which is the highest age limit in the world. Prohibitions typically make things more mysterious for both those who can and cannot consume them. Alcoholic products are no exception. After decades of research, data suggests that while the law has succeeded at reducing overall consumption levels among young people (Wagenaar and Toomey 2000), it has also contributed to binge drinking and to higher consumption levels among college students away from home (Mooney et al. 1992). Much the same logic applies to tobacco products, which in the United States have been required to warn smokers of the dangers of cigarettes since the 1960s. The warning – the manifestation of a law and therefore an institution – changed somehow the product in the package. It has tainted it but also simultaneously encouraged those who dare to use it to think of themselves as rebellious, risk-takers, and perhaps even brave.

Consider, in turn, how regulations affect advertising. Strict laws by the United States Congress and the Federal Trade Commission define what can, cannot, and must be said about pharmaceutical drugs. In the rest of the world (but for New Zealand), by contrast, patients receive most of their information from doctors, since pharmaceutical companies are simply forbidden from advertising prescription drugs directly to consumers (Gregory 2009). When it comes to most consumer and industrial products, in most countries companies can compare their products explicitly to those of their competitors. But there exist considerable differences across countries as to how this can be done and, therefore, as to what sort of associations and information consumers and clients are exposed to. Moreover, even in the most liberal countries, some products (and services) cannot be compared. For instance, charities in the United States cannot make claims about each other's services. All of this makes it very clear that institutions shape in profound ways the objects of our desire.

B. Making Boundaries: Permissible and Impermissible Objects and Exchanges

Markets are spaces where goods are traded, and institutions affect those spaces in two important ways. Most obviously, they set *boundaries* around them, dictating what is allowed inside those spaces and what must be left out. For instance, none of us can walk into a pharmacy or any other store to buy an ounce of cocaine. Certain medicines, in turn, are available over the counter, while others require a physician's prescription. Lots of potentially very fast but unsafe cars cannot be sold and are therefore not produced. And quotas limit the amount of lobsters that can be fished off the coast of Maine. This means that we, as consumers, move in spaces where, unknown to us, certain objects never appear while others are allowed to exist. Laws and regulations set at the federal and state levels shape much of the above. In all but two states in the United States, for instance, laws make prostitution illegal. Where it is legal, as in most of Nevada (but not Las Vegas) and Rhode Island, it can only be practiced in very particular settings. In Nevada it can only happen in brothels while in Rhode Island, where brothels and street prostitution are illegal, it must be practiced in private settings.

Many things, then, are simply left out of the marketplace by way of institutions. But outlawing products and services does not always lead to their disappearance. Cars that do not comply with federal safety requirements are certainly not available in the United States. Yet heroin and cocaine are available throughout the country, as are prostitution in most cities and towns, alcohol in dry counties, and personal loans for theoretically unqualified illegal immigrants (Portes and Sensenbrenner 1993). The black market across nations for arms or ivory is very large as well. As such, informal economies come into being once laws disallow certain products and services from mainstream marketplaces. There, transactions are sometimes executed behind closed doors or in the dark. Sometimes, however, they take place in full daylight – as is the case, for instance, of street vendors in many African countries (Macharia 1997).

Importantly, these informal economies are not rule-free. There exist codes of conduct, which are enforced not by public officials but by private actors (such as drug lords, for instance, or other sorts of powerful or wealthy individuals). Transactions are executed in certain ways. Some behaviors are not allowed, and particular options are available while others are not. Thus, for instance, the enormous labor market for illegal farm workers in California follows rather precise rules when it comes to hiring, firing, and compensation. Many workers also follow established practices when they are in need of medical attention, with an entire black economy in place to cater to them (Sack 2008). Likewise, among New York immigrants from the Dominican Republic and Cuban exiles in Southern Florida, failure to repay loans obtained in the informal market resulted, for many years, in painful ostracism from business circles (Portes and Sensenbrenner 1993).

We may say, therefore, that laws defining what is legitimate ultimately create three types of spaces: formal marketplaces, informal marketplaces, and what we may call a "black hole" where all items that are in fact never produced belong. We may also say that the first two types of spaces are institutionalized internally: they have particular sets of rules and practices, which order and make possible the execution of transactions. In the formal marketplace, there tends to be a mixture of formal and informal rules and practices. In the informal marketplace, most rules and practices are almost by definition informal, though by no means less real or consequential.

The second way in which institutions affect these spaces is by endowing them with certain *properties*. First, these spaces are never fixed. What is left out of one space at one point in time is sometimes allowed later on. This was the case of alcohol during and after Prohibition, various types of pharmaceutical drugs or alternative medicines, certain financial products and services, certain types of foods, gambling, and so on. Such changes happen most directly because of changes in laws. Institutions change. This is what occurred, for instance, in the wake of the 2008–9 financial crisis and the re-regulation of the financial industry. Sub-prime mortgages – widespread before the crisis – all but disappeared in the United States due to new laws set in place by Congress. But behind changes in laws often lie shifts in less formal institutions (for instance, the ways in which interest groups – e.g., bankers – interface with government) and, of course, in the relative power held by interested parties, cultural trends, technology, and other variables. For instance, in many states, acupuncture became legal in the 1970s and 1980s as mainstream media began documenting its positive effects, practitioners organized themselves more forcefully, and curricula in medical schools allowed for some discussion of it.

Second, both formal and informal marketplaces can expand or contract "organically" (i.e., without the inclusion from outside of formally forbidden products, or the expulsion from the marketplace of formally accepted products). Consider the example of intellectual property law. Patents grant those who own them the exclusive rights to certain technologies and products. In the world of pharmaceuticals, this means that competitors wishing to sell drugs for a particular health condition *must* develop alternative formulas. Patent laws thus in a way force the market to become bigger: new drugs and medicines are constantly being invented because of intellectual property considerations. Or consider how the promulgation of Civil Rights legislation from the 1960s on has given rise to a massive new job market for anti-discrimination officers, lawyers, and administrators (Dobbin and Sutton 1998). Or take the example of anti-trust and competition laws. In virtually every capitalist country, governments do not allow monopolies in private sectors of the economy and, as a result, the numbers of competitors multiply. Microsoft was required by the federal government to share its programming codes with third parties to ensure compatibility between its operating systems and those competitors' browsers. No single company can, in turn, dominate the airline industry to the point where it is the only provider of flights. If this happens, the government takes steps to break up that company into smaller competitors – as occurred in the telecommunications industry with AT&T in the early 1980s.

Third, we observe that not all products belonging to the formal marketplace are inevitably available to all consumers there. This is in part because a confluence of institutional dynamics – a mixture of parallel and potentially conflicting rules and practices – applies to the products in question. One law can make a product legal while another law can specify that it is, in fact, illegal for some potential consumers (the most obvious example being alcoholic drinks). But there are also non-state institutions that can overlap with government law. Thus, Kosher-observing Jews all over the world are constantly exposed to foods which secular law recognizes as legitimate but which they are not permitted to consume. Their religious rules and practices clash with those of their governments. Much the same can be said to apply to Hindus and beef, for instance. It is worth noting that non-institutional variables, of course, can also play a major role in determining the selected availability of products to consumers. For example, in areas of conflict (such as Israel and Gaza, or Sudan), at times powerful actors deny to others access to those products.

Finally, we observe great variations across marketplaces as to what actually happens there. Hiring and firing workers can be very easily done in the United States (though state-level laws can vary significantly even there) and Denmark, but not in France. Credit cards are used for purchasing purposes much more often in the United States than in most European countries. It is, in turn, very easy for customers in the United States to return a product if they are not satisfied with it; the same process is much more complicated in Italy. Within a country, we also note great differences. In Australia, the formal acceptance of acupuncturists varies across states (Baer 2006). In the United States, in some neighborhoods one can first pump gas at a station and then pay; in other neighborhoods payment must come first. In addition, we observe variations over time. In the realm of biotechnology, for instance, what can or cannot be patented shifts over the years (Carolan 2008). All these are differences that are due to institutions, though of course political, cultural, and historical variables also play a role.

C. Information: What Consumers Know

A basic assumption of neoclassical economic theory is that information is plentiful, exhaustive in its content, and easily accessible. Under this school of thought, consumers are well aware of most, if not all, of their options. They understand quite well what they want at a particular point in time and the utility (pleasure, uses, etc.) that they can derive from any given option. They also have unfailing clairvoyance about the future – specifically, the extent to, and ways in which, any particular choice is likely to make them happy or not over time. That basic assumption has been questioned by many scholars – many economists included. Economic sociologists as well as anthropologists have been among the most skeptical (Geertz 2001). First, information, in their view, is obviously limited in quantity. They have accordingly set out to understand how, exactly, this is the case and why. In doing so, they have found that institutions play a major role. Second, they have stressed that the information that is in fact available happens to have a specific content. This happens neither naturally nor by chance. Rather, a number of variables – among them institutions – play a major role. Let us consider these ideas in detail.

Limited quantity of information

Consider first what we may call the role of institutions in limiting the quantity of information in the economy. In many markets, customers seldom have abundant data about the goods that they are thinking of purchasing. Instead, the data is partial at best. Do we really know how long a shirt we see at one of The Gap stores will last? Do we have any data on whether the windbreaker we are eyeing at a Banana Republic outlet is truly waterproof? How does the cotton in those shorts that are on sale compare to that in shorts not on sale? What is true for everyday transactions is also true for less frequent but often more consequential transactions. How good will those skis be? How long will that car's engine last for? How well is that house built? With considerable effort, we can improve how much we know. Many of us shop around, conduct searches on the Internet, and ask our friends and relatives for their opinions. But the resulting information is always partial. We could call it fuzzy, incomplete, or filtered.

This is so even when we have the illusion that we have, in fact, plenty of information on hand. When we pick up, for instance, a jar of jam or any other food product, we find nutritional information. The manufacturer lists data on its protein, carbohydrate, fat, and other contents. It lists, as well, its ingredients. But the manufacturer does not inform us of everything that is in that product (for instance, traces of pesticide). When, in turn, we search on the Internet for an airplane ticket for a flight from New York to Los Angeles, most of us are under the impression that we are able to gather pretty much all the information we need. But that is often far from being the case. How many of us know, for example, that prices vary at different days of the week and month with some regularity? Or that some seats that are apparently identical (including in price) are in fact quite different from each other because, to name one factor, legroom in some is restricted by the presence of a box on the floor covering the wiring for the entertainment system? We are altogether missing valuable pieces of information – and are often unaware of being in such a predicament in the first place.

In what ways, then, do institutions limit the quantity of information that is available in the marketplace? Often, standard industry practices – neither legislated nor regulated officially – limit what we can know. Anyone familiar with purchasing a car in the United States, for example, knows very well that prices on dealer lots and window stickers mean very little. Cars do not come with real prices, but with manufacturer "suggested" prices. Consumers hence participate in one of the most important sectors of the American economy while ignorant of the price of the goods before them. Indeed, we may say that those prices do not actually exist in any real sense – for different customers buying the exact same vehicle are very likely to pay different amounts of money.

Many companies have, in turn, non-compete and non-disclosure contracts with their employees. These contracts prevent employees from divulging sensitive information to outsiders about a significant range of issues, such as formulas, methods, techniques, and processes. In the United States, these contracts are regulated at the state, rather than federal, level. However, 46 states have by now adopted the Uniform Trade Secrets Act, which sets out the basic principles behind these contracts. Punishments include injunctions and damage reparations. The Act thus ensures that we, as consumers, know the ingredients of Coca-Cola but are ignorant of the precise mix of those ingredients.

At a more fundamental level, consumers belonging to different class structures and groups are exposed to different institutional environments which themselves affect the information available. In rich neighborhoods, for instance, public and private schools have in place processes and routines that make significant quantities of valuable information available to their constituents. Stronger academic curricula teach young consumers how to discern between healthy and unhealthy foods, a powerful or outdated computer, or the values of different college educations. Something quite different typically happens in poorer neighborhoods. There, weak institutional mechanisms for the distribution of data keep young people relatively in the dark about the world. The same can be said of public libraries and their routine activities and programs in rich versus poor areas. We observe, in other words, an uneven distribution of information throughout society, with significant portions of the population – those with limited resources, power, and knowledge – lacking access to precious information about the world around them.

Now, broader institutional variables explain in good part local institutional realities. Schools in poorer neighborhoods are underfunded as a result of the established practice in the United States of funding public school systems with local property taxes. Under-represented interest groups in society enjoy fewer and weaker channels of access to key lawmakers and policymakers. Furthermore, electoral rules and processes shape political outcomes, fiscal choices, and thus on-the-ground outcomes (such as funding levels for libraries, online resources, etc.) that favor some constituents over others (Hacker and Pierson 2007).

The recent turmoil in the global economy highlights an

additional institutional factor that limits information in the marketplace: the complex nature of contracts that underlie most economic transactions. To this date, few credit card and mortgage consumers understand all of the terms on which they are borrowing money. The language is difficult to grasp and the implications of particular clauses are unclear except to legal experts. Simpler transactions are similarly riddled with language that is difficult to comprehend. Few buyers of airline tickets on online sites such as Orbitz understand the obligations of those merchants or the airlines themselves, such as those that apply to pricing and refund policies.

Specific content of information

Institutions do more, however, than simply limit the quantity of information consumers have available: they directly shape, if not produce, the information that is available. If certain ingredients are listed, for instance, on a jar of jam, it is because federal law in the United States makes that a requirement. Indeed, federal law also states the order in which ingredients ought to be listed, as well as the sort of nutritional information that must be shared (and it also provides guidelines for estimating that information). If providers of medical services must disclose information on the risks and benefits associated with particular drugs or medical procedures, it is because the law requires them to do so. On the consumer side, if real estate buyers must divulge a great deal of their financial information to lenders when applying for a mortgage, it is in great part because of law. It is also due to established industry practices – formal and informal agreements among participants in a given industry to subscribe to certain standards and protocols.

Importantly, note that this is not merely a matter of demanding that certain information flow from providers to consumers and vice versa. It is also often a matter of actually creating that information. For instance, a homebuyer applying for a mortgage may not know with any precision the extent of her financial worth (assets as well as debt). That information must be collected and processed to become available. Similarly, food producers 50 years ago probably did not know the exact caloric or fat content of their goods. Now, they are expected to generate that information. Or, as another example, consider the case of laws and regulations that encourage (by way of funding, tax breaks, or guaranteed initial returns) private actors in the economy to come up with innovative ways and technologies for generating and communicating data about products, services, or manufacturing processes (Block and Keller 2009; Sapat 2004).

On another level, institutions can serve as a conduit or valuable distributor for a specific type of information that is available in some parts of society and could be used in other parts – between sources of information and those looking for information (Streeck 1999). Consider as an illustration what happens on eBay or at the New York Stock Exchange. In both marketplaces information is quite limited. On eBay, buyers and sellers in most transactions do not know each other personally. Buyers – who must pay before receiving the merchandise – fear that sellers will prove unreliable. They lack crucial information about those sellers. At the New York Stock Exchange, traders rely on each other to conduct their transactions, but, again, do not know how trustworthy their peers are. In both cases, institutions have developed to solve these problems. On eBay, buyers have the opportunity to rank sellers on their reliability, punctuality, and other dimensions. Those rankings are made publicly available in a specific format for other potential buyers to see (Kuwabara 2005). Information that existed only in individuals' minds beforehand is now available to all potential buyers. At the New York Stock Exchange, a large number of informal rules dictate what traders can and cannot do, and what they can expect from each other – and repeated compliance with those rules generates trust (Abolafia 2001).

More broadly, governments and a huge number of private institutions have official policies in place to divulge large sets of specific types of data on all sorts of matters related to the economy. For instance, all states – from Alaska to Florida – have extensive, established programs to stimulate tourism in their areas. Many involve specific, detailed initiatives to capture and then make available information on places, events, and much more. The Massachusetts

Office of Travel and Tourism, for example, makes available in printed format (brochures, booklets, etc.) and on its website a wealth of detailed information about Boston Harborfest's Fourth of July celebrations. Across the globe, after receiving significant support by the Taiwanese government to expand their activities to include tourism, farmers have now joined legally sanctioned tourist-oriented associations whose mission includes, among other things, the distribution of information on sites, destinations, and stimulating activities (Lee 2008: 973–4). Tourists interested in visiting farms, picking their own fruits and vegetables, and learning about the lives of farmers now have access to a great deal of useful information.

Note as well that considerable power struggles and bargaining go into determining what data, exactly, is to be presented to the public and thus the sort of institutions that will facilitate or require that process. Different stakeholders logically wish to influence the content of the information that is available, and how, exactly, it is made available and distributed. Each will leverage its resources to ensure that mediators and distributors of information advance its own interests. Their efforts, of course, will themselves be shaped by institutional dynamics. Formal and informal rules and practices determine how stakeholders access the mediators and distributors, and how those mediators and distributors behave toward those stakeholders. Thus, for example, food producers lobbying Congress for the promotion of particular laws will inevitably follow certain procedures for reaching legislators and making their case.

D. *The Flow of Transactions and the Question of Ownership*

Transactions amount to exchanges. Unfolding through time, they can be everything from very simple to very complicated. Going through a toll booth on the highway is a rather straightforward matter. With our cars, we come to a stop as close as possible to the teller, the teller or a sign informs us of the amount due, and a red light or a metal or plastic bar blocks our way. With the window lowered, we hand over some money and, if we gave too much, wait for the change. After that, the light turns green or the bar lifts. In a matter of seconds, we are gone. Purchasing a flight is considerably more complex. After the initial handing over of money – done in the United States typically with a credit card – we must wait days, weeks, or even months before the actual flight. While waiting, dates and times may change. Then, a convoluted set of rituals at the airport takes place: checking in ourselves and perhaps our luggage (including the presentation of officially recognized identification documents), proceeding through security checks, finding our gate, boarding the flight and following numerous instructions, arriving, retrieving our luggage, and finally leaving the airport. Compared to buying a house, however, or relying on a hospital's help to deliver a baby, the required steps are quite simple.

Whether simple or complex, the unfolding of most transactions is orderly: there is a pre-established sequence of events. The parties involved generally know that sequence quite well, so that they almost automatically or semi-consciously participate in it. Such orderliness is critical: if it were missing, exchanges would take far longer. Indeed, they may even not happen at all (Abolafia 2001). If colleges could only offer unclear, unreliable, and ever-changing courses, major requirements, and residential accommodations, many students would hesitate to commit their money to attend them. Likewise, if stock-market investors encountered confusing and ever-shifting guidelines and stipulations from brokerage firms for purchasing and selling stocks, they would probably explore other destinations for their money. Predictability, as Max Weber famously observed, is fundamental for sustained market activity (Weber 1978) and, indeed, for the health and vigor of entire economies (Ginsburg 2000). What, then, makes that order possible? Institutions play an absolutely critical role.

Consider our two examples above. On a toll-way, the deceleration of our cars as we approach the toll booth – the first step in the transaction – is not only a result of good common sense but also of regulation: speed-limit signs order us to slow down. At the same time, the paying of a toll on the highway is something – a practice – that virtually all of us have witnessed since a very young age. We are all quite familiar with it, and it is therefore a routine. Our likely brief exchange of words with the toll collector is not regulated but surely quite scripted. The amount we owe is in turn set by laws (laws, incidentally, which are the products of other sets of institutions, such as the legislative process in that locality). Finally, our release conditional on paying (so that the light turns green or the bar lifts after, not before, we pay) is probably not spelled out in law but left unspecified because the authorities believe (correctly, as it turns out) that most drivers understand the money must first be given before symbols of their release appear before them. We should note, as well, that we trust the teller not to take our money and refuse to release us. Such trust, itself not an institution, is made possible by other institutions – namely, the fact that the teller is subject to a code of conduct which will ensure his dismissal if he acts unprofessionally.

Similar observations apply to our purchase of a flight. Rules dictate how the purchase of a ticket – on the Internet, for example – ought to happen. The government, the credit card company, and the airline itself all contribute their rules. A large number of formal and informal rules and practices, in turn, guide us as we make our way into the airport, the plane, and the arrival site. As we check in, for instance, we stay in line (an essential, informal practice for the speedy and effective processing of passengers). Our pilots will follow an elaborate, routine check of the aircraft before taking off. Everything has to comply with rules. Once moving, they will be instructed countless times on when and where to take off, how high to fly, and much more. Rules and established practices, then, make the orderly flow of transactions possible. Whether formal or informal, they inform actors of what must, and most likely will, happen at a particular point in time. They exclude as inappropriate and impossible particular behaviors and actions. In one word, they structure economic exchanges and thus make them possible.

Interestingly, as it turns out, institutions actually play a bigger role than structuring economic events between buyers and sellers. They also set the preconditions that are necessary for the unfolding of those events. Most fundamentally, if actors did not own anything, most of our transactions (as we know them in our society) would not take place. Buyers would not own money, and sellers would not own goods and services. There would be nothing to structure. In fact, we live in societies where people own money and all sorts of physical and abstract goods, companies own goods and services, federal and state governments own highways, bookstores own books, restaurant owners own food, and so on. Property, in other words, exists and can be owned: private property exists. In addition, private property can be transferred: we recognize, as a matter of law and practice, that one can dispose of property and others can come into its possession – a concept that we can call the "alienability" of private property. What makes private property and its alienability possible? It is a set of institutions that regulate and confer to people, organizations, and other entities the ownership of things: property rights.

Entire books have been written about the nature and evolution of property rights. While we cannot possibly cover them all here, we can discuss a few crucial aspects briefly. First, property rights vary across geographies in ways that do not only reflect efficiency (Anderson and McChesney 2003). Different societies have quite different understandings of what powers and limitations come with "owning" something. History, culture, politics, and even religion – to name some of the most important factors – drive these differences (Carruthers and Ariovich 2004). Different countries regulate differently, for instance, how parents can pass on, as inheritance, money to their children. Within the United States, states vary in how they regulate who can own a gun, how and under what circumstances firearms can be used in public spaces (parks, schools, etc.), when and how firearms may be concealed, and so on. As a whole, the United States has a more liberal regulatory approach to firearms than many other countries. But when it comes to other matters, other countries grant owners more powers than in the United States. Owning a dog, for instance, in many jurisdictions in the United States does not confer owners the right to eat that dog. The same applies in Hong Kong. But in mainland China, a person who owns a dog can, if she so wishes, eat it. In any given society, moreover, property rights change over time. Towns are constantly revisiting their zoning laws, for example, with implications for whether business owners can expand or remodel their buildings.

Second, public authorities, such as federal, state, and city governments, are nowadays typically the source of property rights. They are the ones to create and regulate them (Campbell and Lindberg 1990). Not so long ago, however, private actors had considerably more control over those rights. Feudal lords, powerful army lords, tribal leaders, and others controlled who could own what, what could be owned, the powers and limitations associated with ownership, and much more. Religious authorities also controlled – and do so to this day in some geographies, such as Iran, for instance – those rights.

Third, property rights are distributed rather unevenly in any society, across societies, and over time. During the Cold War, states in communist and socialist countries owned significant portions of the economy and thus of revenues and profits. In Native American societies prior to the arrival of European colonizers, individuals were not allowed to own land: only the community as a whole could (Carruthers and Ariovich 2004: 34 and 26). In feudal Europe and for centuries in the United States, serfs and slaves were in a legal position to own essentially nothing. "The fundamental feature of slavery, in law," wrote Patterson, "was the fact that the slave could not be a proprietor" (Patterson 1982: 182). We observe, moreover, important differences between foreigners and citizens or residents in any given society. The former are at times not allowed to own real estate, for example. There are then enduring and major differences across the genders. In many parts of the developing world, by either law or practice, women have limited access to real estate, money, cars, and much more. Indeed, let us recall that even in Western societies not so long ago women became property of men upon marriage and were thus deprived of the chance to own anything of significance. These uneven distributions of property rights amount, of course, to unequal levels of power held by different actors. Existing institutional arrangements almost always favor some actors over others.

E. Parties in the Exchange

Many students borrow money to attend college. The government, banks, private individuals, and others agree to lend them money at a particular interest rate. Many students work on campuses as well, often in work-study positions. They agree to sell their labor in return for money. In both cases, the students participate in the transactions "as" college students: that is their role in the exchange. If they were not college students, they would not qualify for the money or positions. When a person is sick, in turn, and he visits a physician's office, he meets with nurses and doctors. If the patient were presented with a car mechanic instead, he would not agree to be examined. These examples illustrate a fundamental aspect of economic transactions: exchanges do not happen among anonymous, undefined parties spontaneously interested, somehow, in each other's products and services. This may have been the image of the marketplace that Adam Smith depicted for us in his eighteenth-century classic *Inquiry into the Nature and Causes of the Wealth of Nations* (2000) and that later economists, such as Milton Friedman (1980), espoused. It is simply not accurate.

Buying and selling often happens, instead, among parties endowed with a particular identity, such as that of the student or of the doctor (Spillman 1999). That identity is often recognized, and indeed belongs to, the public sphere: a person "takes on" the identity of a student or doctor. Matters could hardly be otherwise. As buyers, we wish to know without too much effort the identities of the sellers before us. We acquire a great deal of information when we hear that they are insurance agents, car mechanics, or loan specialists. As sellers, in turn, we wish to know that the person before us is a legitimate buyer, capable not only of paying but also of understanding the basic terms of agreement that may accompany the exchange. Identities provide us with very useful informational shortcuts.

Identities, then, are inherent parts of many economic transactions. We may say that without them those transactions would not occur, and that they certainly would not occur in the fashion that they do. The crucial question becomes, then, how parties acquire their identities. How do individuals go from undefined entities to specific, defined parties in an exchange? What mechanisms are involved? Once again, we observe a variety of institutional dynamics at work.

First consider the examples of students taking out loans for their education or new residents in a town signing up for Internet service. In both instances, the individuals are "students" and "residents" before entering into the transaction. Their identities were constituted prior to the exchange. The same can be said of farmers selling their produce in a town market, shoe cobblers in the town square, and even of firms and other organizations constituted by two or more people (such as a law firm, for instance, or a veterinary clinic with two or more partners) who sell their services to individual customers. They were farmers, cobblers, and firms before someone decided to buy their products or services. What, then, made their identities possible? In many cases, formal agreements produced those identities. A person becomes a college student by accepting an offer of admission by a college. A person becomes a town resident when purchasing a home or signing a rental lease. And a law firm comes into being when the partners agree to bring it into existence. Simply put, formal agreements create economic identities (Stryker 2003).

But formal agreements are not the only way individuals acquire their economic identities. A second, major way is to fulfill a set of obligations through time – such as training, coursework, or internships. Those obligations can in some cases be very challenging (for instance, medical or law school) or relatively less demanding (for example, real estate license programs or barber school). They can take little time (as is the case when taking the Certified Public Accountant Examination) or take years (such as a doctorate program in physics). Meeting those obligations translates into certifications, diplomas, degrees and the like – all of which are usually awarded by someone in a position of authority. A person thus "becomes" an accountant not by signing a piece of paper (as is the case for students accepting admission into a college), but by fulfilling a set of publicly recognized requirements.

Yet formal processes are not always required for the acquisition of an economic identity. Management consultants and restaurant waiters – to name two rather different professions – become so not by undergoing a specific type of formal training and being recognized by sources of authority, but, rather, by practical exposure to, and compliance with, established (but by no means regulated or standardized) procedures, codes, and guidelines that are associated with a particular job. Those procedures, codes, and guidelines can be rather unclear and vary by location (different restaurants, for instance, offer very different training programs). Professional associations may issue some recommended standards, while, in some cases, optional certification programs may be available. This lack of formality can sometimes detract from the stability of the identities in question: while there is no question, for instance, that a person with a medical degree is forever a doctor, one could ask whether a waiter who stops working in that position can be considered a waiter indefinitely.

We have so far talked about economic identities that are established prior to economic exchanges. We should now recognize that in many types of exchanges the transaction itself contributes to the constitution of the actors. When one joins a fitness club, that person agrees to become a "member" of the club and, in that function, is in a position to go through the transaction. When a person buys a house from another person, the purchase or sales agreement identifies the parties involved as "buyers" and "sellers." And when someone secures a loan from a bank, he becomes the "borrower." While contracts are often the tools that assign specificity to the parties involved, informal venues are also at times at work. In many developing economies as well as developed ones, many transactions are executed outside the boundaries of the formal economy. Contracts are not drawn up and informal agreements are used instead. These agreements produce identities in their own right. When a guitar teacher agrees to provide someone with private lessons, the recipient of the lessons takes on the identity of guitar student. And when illegal immigrants in California are hired informally by plantation owners to pick strawberries, those immigrants take on the identity of strawberry pickers.

Now, as is the case with institutions in general, the institutions shaping the identity of economic actors are neither predetermined nor given. Power structures, cultural, historical, technological, and other factors influence those institutions. Thus, the curriculum for medical schools (i.e., what obligations one must meet to become a doctor) constantly change over time in response to new research findings, lobbying, dominant standards for truth, and other variables. Primary care physicians must now learn far more about nutrition, for instance, than they did 50 years ago. New medical specializations, in turn, are routinely established in response not only to new empirical evidence but also to shifts in how illnesses and diseases are understood and interpreted. And new categories of "patients" are created and enter the marketplace in response to the ideas and power of medical associations, pharmaceutical companies, patient groups, and other stakeholders in the health industry.

At the same time, not everyone is allowed to take on particular identities via the necessary institutional venues. Exclusionary practices are widespread. We see this in higher education, where most programs (whether at the college or graduate level) discriminate on the basis of academic qualifications, extracurricular activities, test scores, and sometimes geography. We also observe this in a great number of industries where established actors mobilize to prevent others from participating in the marketplace. In the wine industry of France, for instance, not everyone is allowed to be a producer of Appellations d'Origine Contrôlée wines. One must instead meet very specific production methods, geographical considerations, and other requirements – all of which are set out through political struggles, conflicting interpretations of culture and tradition, and more. If excluded, of course, some actors are likely to come together and seek to start new associations and partnership – all with their own institutional characteristics – to advance their interests and possibly exclude others (Garcia-Parpet 2008).

Thus, finally, entire categories of buyers and sellers must sometimes take action to ensure their identities are recognized by formal authorities in the first place. This has certainly been the case recently with "organic" food producers all over the world – who sought differentiation (i.e., their own identity) vis-à-vis other producers – and, going back further in time, with insurance providers and even producers and buyers of consumer products such as bicycles (Burr 2006). All economic identities must be crafted at some point or another – they must emerge. This process generally requires coordination and pressure – for ultimately others must recognize them as legitimate.

F. The Making of Preferences

Consumers approach markets with certain preferences in mind. Standard economic theory takes preferences as starting points. Given certain preferences, and given certain prices, options, and so on, economists model the likely behavior of consumers, sellers and, in the aggregate, entire marketplaces. But a complete understanding of economic transactions cannot ignore the origins of preferences. Preferences do not magically appear into people's minds. They must form. How does this happen? What forces contribute to their making? We must also recognize that preferences are mutable – that they change over time. This is the case for individual people over time but also, in the aggregate, for groups of people. For instance, 80 years ago very few people in the United States were interested in buying life insurance. Today, many more people are.

Psychologists can, of course, shed considerable light on the formation of preferences and their variations over time. Their focus, however, is likely to be on the internal workings of people's minds. Sociologists, on the other hand, emphasize that people function in contexts – cultural, political, historical, and, of course, institutional. It is their belief that those contexts have a profound impact on people's preferences. One's status in society, for instance, heavily shapes the goods and services desired (Blau et al. 1985; Bourdieu 1984). In this section, we consider some of the most important institutional factors.

Let us begin with those institutions which set the broad context in which preferences are formed. These institutions typically affect us by eliminating from our purview certain possibilities and presenting us with others. They do not directly influence how we generate our preferences, but instead make it more or less likely that we develop certain preferences over others. Examples include state policies and laws that encourage the development of certain industries, such as pharmaceuticals or high technology. The state of Massachusetts, for instance, has long pushed for the growth of those two industries along its Route 128 corridor and elsewhere. Currently, the government of China is promoting – via fiscal and financial incentives – the growth of clean-technology products and services. These types of initiatives have had a major impact on job creation, higher education programs, and even the attractiveness of certain cities and neighborhoods over others. How has all of this affected preference formation and change over time? They have shaped individuals' views of their careers, their desires of what educational institutions to attend, and what a good apartment or house should look like. While 50 years ago a person would have considered farming or low-tech manufacturing as an option, he is now much more likely to contemplate rather different venues. State policies and laws shape what we work toward and why, as Hirschman (1977) famously noted for capitalism at large.

At a more local level, consider the practice of funding public schools, in part, with local property taxes – something that happens in the United States, for example, but not in several European countries. The federal government of the United States contributes funds that cover less than 10 percent of the overall costs of public education. Reliance on local resources has led to major inequalities in schools. High schools in particular exercise great influence over students' understanding of the world. In a well-funded high school, students are exposed to a wealth of information about colleges, computers, athletics, and the world in general. Their preferences as consumers in society are affected by these broader considerations. Similar observations apply to a great variety of markets and environments. For instance, as Wonders and Michalowski (2001) showed, laws, lobbying patterns, state-industry regulations, immigration regulations, and other institutions influence the evolution of the prostitution industry in any given setting. Different prostitution practices develop accordingly in those settings. Those differences, in turn, shape in broad terms how sex tourists conceive of different destinations, their fantasies, and ultimately what they wish for as they reach their destinations. Thus, sex tourists in Amsterdam – where prostitution is legal, organized and practiced as a physical and commercial transaction above all, and now involves migrant women as well as Dutch ones – are looking for primarily a physical experience in a well-regulated environment: with money in their pockets, they go "shopping for bodies" as they would for any other service or good. In Havana – where prostitution remains illegal – formally or informally organized brothels do not exist, and women working more independently approach the rich tourists from abroad in a more personal and romantic fashion. Here, tourists are hoping for a more intimate, more ambiguous, and almost emotional experience, one in which they see themselves as travelers from distant, well-off countries falling in love with exotic girls from a poorer, though more sensuous, place.

But institutional factors can also be more directly involved with the making and changing of preferences. Indeed, they are sometimes designed specifically to influence those preferences. For instance, tax laws covering mortgage interest deductions affect how people feel about purchasing a home. The passage of a first-time home-buyer tax credit during the 2008–9 financial crisis spurred many people to conceive, for the first time, of owning a home. Note that some of these individuals certainly wanted to buy a house and the change in law permitted them to do so – that is, their preferences did not change. For other people, however, the tax credit prompted them to entertain in their minds something new. The same thing can be said about usury laws setting interest rate ceilings. If those ceilings are lowered, consumers begin to think about owning something that was before beyond their reach and therefore imagination.

Or think about the impact of sumptuary laws – laws that attempt to regulate habits of consumption when it comes to things like food and clothing – throughout the centuries and across most of the world. Between the fifteenth and seventeenth centuries especially, European authorities regulated through legal means what people could wear, eat, and surround themselves with. The level of detail was astounding. This is what an English statute from 1533 pronounced:

> None but the King and Royal Family shall wear purple silk, or cloth of gold tissue . . . First, that no person or persons of what estate, dignity, or degree or condition soever they be . . . use or wear in any manner of their apparel or upon their horse, mule, or any other beast any silk of the colour of purple, nor any cloth of gold tissue, but only the King, Queen, the King's mother, the King's children, the King's brothers and sisters, and the King's uncles and aunts; except that it shall be lawful to all Dukes and Marquises to wear and use in their doublets and sleeveless coats, cloth of gold tissue and in no other of their garments, so that the same to be worn by such Dukes and Marquises shall not exceed the price of £5 a yard.
>
> . . . And it is also enacted that no men under the estate of a Duke, Marquis, Earl, and their children, or under the degree of Baron, unless he be a Knight that is Companion of the Garter, from the said Feast, wear in any part of his apparel any woollen cloth made out of this realm of England, Ireland, Wales, Calais, Berwick, or the marches of the same, except in bonnets. (Quoted in Hunt 1996: 411)

The direct impact of the statute on the royal family can be easily imagined (they all wanted to wear purple silk, cloths of gold tissues, and woolen clothes). The impact on the rest of the population can be readily guessed: most probably fancied all things purple, and whoever could afford it used as much wool in their bonnets as possible. Sumptuary laws covered much more than what royalties could or could not do: they affected entire populations, and they did so throughout the world. They existed in colonial America, Japan from the early 1600s to the late 1800s, ancient Rome, China for 15 centuries until the 1500s, and elsewhere. Today, sumptuary laws are mostly gone, though notable vestiges remain. Laws banning smoking and the use of drugs in the United States, and religious laws in some Islamic countries – such as Saudi Arabia – on how women should be dressed in public are important examples.

A plethora of routines and shared assumptions about the world, in turn, directly shape individuals and their economic preferences. Consider two examples from the financial services industry, which today reaches millions of consumers. While hardly anyone felt the need or impulse to purchase life insurance 100 years ago, now millions of individuals buy life insurance every year. How did all these people become interested in quantifying, rationalizing, and calculating in monetary terms their own deaths? Savvy and powerful lobbying, helpful regulation, demographic changes, and urbanization – along with other trends – combined early in the twentieth century to create new norms and expectations about parents, children, life, and immortality (Zelizer 1978). Over the years, a new model for "good" and "conscientious" parents – people who look after their own children in death as well as in life – emerged, became institutionalized, and spread throughout society.

Analogous dynamics took place in the area of personal retirement. Many adults in the developed world today spend enormous resources estimating, preparing for, and imagining their retirement years. About 200 years ago, very few people gave retirement any serious thought at all. Indeed there was no conception of "retirement" as a life phase for individuals. Now, most people approach it with very strong desires and wishes. Why such a dramatic change? What accounts for the new "preferences" of adults in countries such as the United States, Japan, or France? Retirement has become institutionalized. We recognize it as a period of self-fulfillment, relaxation, ambition, and joy and, as such, it has become an important part of our lives. And, as with life insurance, a number of variables account for its institutionalization. The rise of the modern nation-state and, with it, of the individual as the primary actor in society, was particularly crucial in this process (Mayer and Schoepflin 1989: 193–4). In the case of the United States, industry players have pushed the federal government to recognize tax-exempt, actively managed retirement plans such as 401Ks and Individual Retirement Accounts. Many companies offer such plans to their employees, with an army of financial advisors and money managers catering to (and benefiting from) individuals and their planning. The result is simple: those of us who neglect to take retirement seriously are likely to be judged as foolish and as headed for a troubled old age.

Conclusion

Individuals engage in economic exchanges in often seamless fashion. Most transactions seem to happen almost spontaneously, with individuals interested in something looking around and finding someone who is keen on selling it. The appearance of simplicity belies a complex, socially constructed reality.

The objects of our desires, rather than existing naturally, are laden with attributes we as a society project upon, or "inject" into, them. Their existence in the marketplace or the informal economy is far from being natural. As we contemplate our choices and move about in the marketplace, specific amounts and types of information shape our perception of the world around us while other data never reaches us. For every exchange, we follow a specific sequence of actions and reactions, and come away somehow secure that we own (or have parted from) the objects in question, have sold our labor, have acquired someone else's services, and so on. If asked, we recognize that, in fact, the people around us are not anonymous individuals but doctors, bank tellers, insurance agents, and coffee-shop owners. If probed further, we may become cognizant that our preferences did not just happen to be in our heads but somehow came to us – that they grew and developed inside our heads, sometimes quickly but more often slowly and over many years.

In this chapter, we learned that institutions contribute in profound ways to the creation of this complex and subtle economic reality. Institutions mold the world around and inside us. They contribute to the "making" of products, market boundaries, information, transaction steps, parties in exchanges, and our very preferences. Their impact is multifold and varied. Sometimes they are intimately and causally connected to the economic reality we observe. At other times, they provide the broader context in which economic activity unfolds.

Institutions are not the only variables at work, of course. We have seen that they interact with other factors – such as culture, politics, power, and history. We have also learned that different countries offer different institutional environments and, additionally, that the institutional environment in any given country changes over time. We can nonetheless talk about the independent impact of institutions. It is enormous and of great consequence to the economic lives of individuals, and it can be conceptually isolated and dissected. In the next chapter, we will leave individuals behind and focus on organizations and their economic behavior. There, too, we will see that institutions play a profound role in both making things possible as well as shaping what takes place.

3

Organizations

Organizations play an enormous role in modern societies. Firms, business associations, hospitals, insurance companies, interest groups, leagues and clubs, unions, and schools – to name a few – affect the daily life of every member of society. The economic behavior of organizations refers to those actions and processes that organizations undertake or follow in order to acquire, manage, and distribute resources. How do organizations – for instance, the pharmaceutical company Pfizer or the University of Texas at Austin – structure themselves internally to attain their objectives? How do they go about defining their objectives in the first place? What sort of valuable knowledge and information do they gather and share internally? Economists have typically answered these questions in terms of efficiency. Organizations engage in those actions and processes that ensure the most success for the least cost. Sociologists think otherwise. In their view, institutions, rather than efficiency, can account for many of the actions and processes that we observe across organizations.

We can differentiate between institutions operating outside and inside organizations. Institutions *outside* of organizations are at work at various levels: globally, nationally, and within what scholars call "organizational fields." They include regulations, standards, and policies promulgated by supranational bodies, states, transnational organizations, and international industry associations. They also include more informal and less visible institutions, such as non-binding norms, processes, and dominant models and blueprints in world society. Institutions at work *inside* organizations can operate independently of, or in conjunction with, institutions found outside organizations. Among them, we find protocols and regulations that filter knowledge and information originating from outside or inside of organizations, norms and codes of conduct guiding everyday behavior, and myths – or sets of internalized principles about the appropriate actions and processes that any serious organization should follow or engage in.

Figure 3.1 identifies some of the most important institutions we explore in this chapter and their impact on organizational actions and processes. A few key lessons will emerge as we proceed in our analysis. Institutions generate inertia, put a premium on legitimacy, affect the formulation of problems and solutions, and both limit and generate options. The result may be economic behavior that is less than efficient but that is often desirable nonetheless, for organizations gain greater stability, access to more resources, and a clearer sense of direction. Additionally, we will see that, through various mechanisms that have little to do with efficiency, institutions pressure organizations operating in a given organizational field (higher education, for instance, or health care) toward conformity in actions and processes – or toward what sociologists call isomorphism. Because of institutional dynamics, organizations (colleges or hospitals, for example) in a given organizational field look very much alike. All this will provide us with a very useful way of accounting for the economic behavior of organizations – one that has largely been ignored by economists and other observers of organizations. Table 3.1 identifies some of the most important concepts we will encounter in this chapter.

We begin by examining the institutions that operate outside of organizations – for these surround and set the broader context in which organizations function. We then turn to those operating inside organizations. In the section before the conclusion, we investigate closely the concept of isomorphism: given that isomorphism happens, can we categorize in some way the sorts of institutional mechanisms that drive organizations toward conformity?

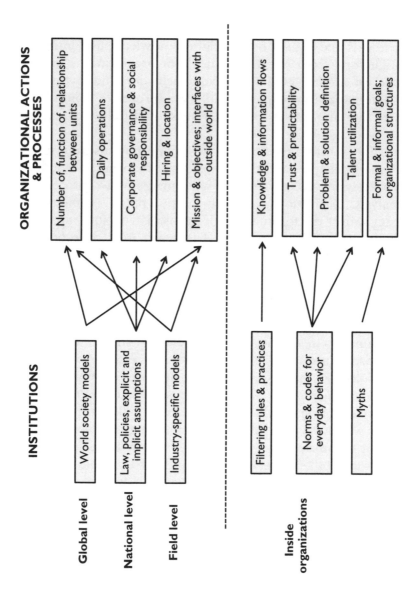

Figure 3.1 Institutions and organizations

Table 3.1   Key concepts for the economic behavior of organizations

Key concept	Definition
Models	Real-life organizations or abstract sets of principles setting standards for the actions and processes of other organizations
Filtering institutions	Practices and rules affecting the flow of information and data within and across organizational boundaries
Legitimacy	Organizational conformity with expected, though not necessarily efficient, actions and processes
Stickiness	Tendency of institutions to change slowly, if at all
Isomorphism	Organizations in a given field exhibiting very similar actions and processes

A. *Institutions Outside of Organizations*

Institutions outside of organizations influence the actions and processes of those organizations as they acquire, manage, and distribute resources (Scott 2008a). We consider first those institutions operating at the global level.

Global-level institutions

In the late nineteenth century, Japan sent various delegations to major Western societies in order to learn about and emulate their parliaments, police forces, and armies. In the aftermath of World War II, manufacturing and service companies in Europe turned to the United States for clues on how to structure successful businesses. After the fall of the Soviet Union, government officials and scholars from Western, capitalistic countries mobilized, often at the request of the recipient countries, to export their supposedly superior principles of political and economic management to the newly freed nations and republics. Today, in Russia and Eastern Europe more generally, new business schools and universities are established with departmental structures, curricula, and objectives that closely resemble those of business schools and universities in Western Europe and the United States.

What do these examples tell us? There exist in world society dominant models of what organizations should look like: their mission and objectives, administrative units, basic relationships among those units, public profiles, and so on. Often, specific organizations are seen as leading examples of those models. In the world of management consulting, for instance, this might be McKinsey & Company. In higher education, it might be Harvard University. And in the realm of welfare government programs, it might be the Scandinavian countries. Dominant models are seen as "modern," "universal," and "rational" (Strang and Meyer 1994; Jepperson and Meyer 1991; Meyer 1994). As such, they are believed to be superior to the alternatives and new public- and private-sector organizations feel compelled to embrace those models. Old organizations are either reformed or, if that proves impossible, dismantled. Virtually every major corporation in the world today, for instance, has human resources departments that, on paper, seek to attract and manage the "best talent" regardless of gender or race. A great number of nation-states in the twentieth century, in turn, established extensive laws and environmental ministries in response to expectations in world society that a modern nation-state is responsible, at once, for economic growth and the protection of the environment (Frank et al. 2000).

The impact of dominant models reaches beyond the internal constitution of organizations and extends to their interface with outside actors, such as the state, suppliers, and customers. They do so by offering instructions about the relevant policies, procedures, public profiles, and data systems that organizations should have (Marchionini 2002). No major company today, for instance, can afford to operate without an Internet website specifying its missions, products and services, contact information, and locations. This is in part because websites can help business in a traditional sense: more potential customers can learn about the company, new products and services can be more readily announced, and so on. But it is also because failure to have a website would signal that something is "wrong" about the company in question: that it is disconnected, anachronistic, and backwards. In one word, the legitimacy of the company (and perhaps even its existence) would come into question. In the case of nation-states and their environmental objectives and thus laws, for instance, "an identifier or label of oddness follows whenever a country violates them. Imagine a country without any national parks or nature reserves. It would definitely be regarded as strange, perhaps even unqualified to be a nation-state" (Song 2008: 31).

Where do dominant models come from? Large-scale political, cultural, and economic factors play a role. At the end of World War II, because of who won and lost the conflict, American-style corporate capitalism emerged as the perceived best way to organize economies and firms. The approach emphasized anti-trust regulations, professional ownership and leadership, and mass production and formalization (Djelic 1998). When the West prevailed in the Cold War, Western firms (and especially, again, those from the United States) became instant standard-setters. But powerful transnational and international bodies also play a major role (Boli and Thomas 1997). Organizations like the International Labor Rights Fund, the World Wide Fund for Nature, and Greenpeace articulate and project onto the globe guidelines and instructions for organizational behavior. There are guidelines for how organizations should treat their workers, the environment, and the broader community (Bartley 2003). The United Nations and associations of scientists, in turn, have produced white papers, declarations, and recommendations about the need for nation-states, as organizations, to devote resources to the protection of the environment. Yet national-level actors also at times contribute to the formulation of global models. *Times Higher Education,* for instance, issues yearly rankings of the world's top 200 universities. The ones at the pinnacle, of course, represent the ideal. The rankings are closely monitored worldwide by the public, politicians, professionals, and others.

We see transnational and international bodies at work in the realm of corporate governance as well. What powers should the board of directors have? What about the shareholders or workers? An emerging model at the global level is the stakeholder-oriented paradigm, which puts more power in the hands of workers than has traditionally been the case. The EU has been instrumental in generating that model by issuing two important and mandatory (for its member-states) laws on the matter: the Acquired Rights Directive (ARD) and the Collective Redundancies Directive (CRD). The directives give employees a voice in their respective organizations in the event of a transfer of business ownership between employers during restructuring or large collective layoffs (Armour and Deakin 2003). Employers must now inform and consult employee representatives about their decisions.

The practical impact of these models is often considerable. For instance, the ARD and CRD affected BMW's proposed sale of Rover to Alchemy Partners in the UK – a sale that would have caused the loss of approximately 24,000 jobs (Armour et al. 2003). Claims made by employee representatives that the proposal contravened provisions mandated by the ARD and CRD ultimately redirected the sale to the Phoenix consortium – Alchemy Partners' rival bidders. Rover escaped being significantly downsized, maintained its role as a volume car producer, saved millions of dollars, and also minimized the number of dismissals it had to make. Major retailers, such as The Gap, have changed their sourcing practices significantly as a result of "shaming" campaigns by watchdogs exposing them as failing to comply with expectations. Nation-states all over the globe have poured significant resources into environmental programs. It is clearly difficult and risky to ignore dominant models in world society.

At the same time, dominant models do not always and inevitably impose themselves onto organizations. This is the case even for those models that put forth legally mandatory principles, such as those coming from the EU and the WTO, and those that incorporate principles that may not be binding but can be costly to ignore, such as those coming from the IMF or World Bank. Not every organization faithfully subscribes to all aspects of dominant models. Indeed, most of them do not. Differences in interpretation, the extent of "fit" with local organizational culture and structures, the possibility of competing models, and the degree to which dominant global models may in fact hamper daily operations in a given organization are among the most important reasons for the persistence of old patterns and behaviors. Also important is the ability of affected constituents to mobilize for or against the adoption of a model – that is, to exert their own power over the articulation of what should be followed by all. In the case of post-World War II Europe, for instance, well-positioned business leaders in France and West Germany objected – sometimes with the help of powerful trade unions – to aspects of the American corporate model (Djelic 1998). Thus, dominant models surely pressure organizations worldwide toward conformity, but the adoption of those models is never absolute.

National-level institutions

Much research has been conducted on how national institutions influence the strategies, internal procedures, and structure of organizations. Many of these institutions originate from the state in the form of laws and policies, but others are more informal or indirect. We examine here the impact of institutions on four major types of actions and processes: corporate governance, corporate social responsibility, hiring from the labor market, and the choice of physical location for offices and plants.

Let us turn, first, to corporate governance – or the principles and customs that define how corporations are controlled and directed. In themselves, these are institutions. In any given country, we are likely to observe similar corporate governance practices. Why is this the case? Most countries have formal laws and regulations in place to protect the interests of shareholders or employees. The legal system in Japan grants shareholders broad voting powers, while in the United States corporate regulation provides protection for individual minority shareholders through measures like strong disclosure requirements. In other countries, representation rights give employees certain decision-making powers in their firms. Company law in Germany, France, China, and the Netherlands, for instance, either requires or permits listed firms to have a two-tiered board comprising of a Board of Management and a Supervisory Board (where employees are included) charged with monitoring managers. Behind these regulatory differences lie other country-level institutional variables, such as existing conceptions and regulations about property rights (Aguilera and Jackson 2003).

The extent of influence that legal institutions have on corporate governance can vary, of course, especially if they are not enforceable or if other corporate practices interfere with and mediate their effectiveness. In the United States, although company law grants shareholders the ability to elect their board members in order to monitor companies' decision-makers, this system does not work out as well in practice, given that management generally chooses the list of nominees (Aguilera 2005). Furthermore, as shareholders are often limited to voting "yes" or abstaining from voting, the proposals that management puts forward for the election of directors will still pass even if most of the voters abstain. In Germany, while codetermination is aimed at giving employees a voice in the company, rich stockholders often have ways of silencing those voices and advancing their own interests instead (Roe 2006).

Interestingly, once corporate governance structures are established, organizations have a tendency to hold on to these structures, even when there may not be any legal mandate to do so. Put differently, governance structures become deeply institutionalized, grow sticky, and adhere to the organizations that adopt them – much as it happens for other sorts of regulatory frameworks and practices, such as operating standards and procedures (Tate 2001). In their study of foreign firms listing their stocks in American stock markets, for instance, Davis and Marquis (2005) found that most of the firms did not adopt American governance practices either before or after establishing a presence in the United States. Except for the new Israeli firms whose headquarters were already established in the United States or which were funded by Americans who then served on their boards, foreign firms did not generally gravitate toward American practices by incorporating small boards or more accessible disclosure practices into their organizational make-up. Instead, most maintained the governance structures of their home countries. Still, we should also note that change can and does happen at times, as Culpepper (2010) recently showed, for instance, in his penetrating analysis of Japanese and French corporations, and the revisions they underwent in response to the introduction of new national laws that, in a deviation from the past, allow investors to sell and buy corporations even when this goes against the preferences of senior management. But even so, when change does happen, we see that it is seldom abrupt: there is quite often some degree of continuity with past practices (Goyer 2011).

Informal, nation-wide institutional variables also influence corporate governance structures in any given country. These include explicit and implicit collections of principles and norms about the appearance and behavior of organizations (Thornton and Ocasio 1999). These informal institutions are often as stable as more formal ones, though they, too, inevitably change over time (Scott 2008b). They often interact with more formal institutions as well. The practice of stock repurchase plans illustrates this (Zajac and Westphal 2004). In the mid-1980s, established assumptions about managers began to change, following the rising dissatisfaction with how large American firms had been performing since the mid-1970s. While managers were once valued for, and believed to have, the expertise and knowledge to allocate resources efficiently, their image began to shift toward one of self-interested actors who looked out for their own interests at the cost of those of shareholders. New informal guidelines for how to treat managers thus began to emerge. Soon, they were followed by formal policies and incentive plans targeted at bridging the interests of managers and shareholders. Stock repurchase plans – which shifted free cash flows from managers back to investors through the firm's repurchase and retirement of part of its shares – were put into place in many corporations.

Let us now turn to corporate social responsibility. Socially responsible corporations seek to have, as they pursue their business objectives, positive effects on society. Here "society" refers to entities and things both outside (i.e., the environment) and inside (i.e., employees) of corporations. Acting in a socially responsible manner may, in certain cases, be economically beneficial for corporations. Yet simple profit calculations (which may or may not be in fact accurate) are often not the only variable driving such behavior. National institutions, such as laws, have for some time pressured companies to act in a responsible manner (Gjølberg 2009; Campbell 2007). In the United States, since the enactment of the Civil Rights Act of 1964, federal policy has heavily intervened in the area of employment rights (Dobbin and Sutton 1998). Legislation has extended to equal employment opportunity and benefits, and health and safety. Laws have not been very specific, however, partly because the Constitution of the United States limits Congressional reach into the private sector. The resulting ambiguity has pressured corporations and other organizations to create special procedures to ensure compliance with a wide range of possible demands, and to set up specialized departments for interpretation and compliance (Sutton et al. 1994; Kalev et al. 2006). Experts, in turn, have legitimated and supported the creation and diffusion of these new departments.

More informal institutions – some of which, one could point out, are almost cultural in nature – have also been at work. In Japan, for instance, tacit assumptions about lifelong employment for workers have profoundly impacted the strategies of Japanese firms both in good and poor economic times (Westney 2001). During the recession of the 1990s and the first decade of the new millennium, Japanese managers hesitated to dismiss workers, and opted instead to cut costs by reducing recruitment, eliminating management bonuses, doing away with overtime hours, and creating offshoot enterprises where employees could continue to work. Quite the opposite can be said of the United States, where massive layoffs are the norm during economic crises. Countries also differ in terms of the processes and mechanisms through which different industry and interest groups communicate, bargain, and reach agreements about what corporations should do to be socially responsible (Campbell 2007: 954). Consensus building practices are widespread in Scandinavian countries, for instance, while more confrontational practices are the norm in the United States and the United Kingdom. These differences shape the choices and behavior of corporations.

Private and public associations, in turn, have instituted programs and events that pressure organizations to act in a socially responsible manner. For years, for example, the Minneapolis Chamber of Commerce promoted corporate giving through the Two and Five Percent Club (Galaskiewicz 1991). At the club's annual awards luncheon, Chamber of Commerce members who gave either 2 percent or 5 percent of their pre-tax profits to charities were given awards publicly before political officials and members of the public and press. A number of environmental organizations publicly rank and give out awards to corporations for their use of resources and efforts to control pollution. Other organizations, such as City Year, enter into partnerships with corporations (such as Pepsi, for instance) to pursue specific goals (such as community service in poor neighborhoods to help disadvantaged children succeed).

Consider now how organizations interact with the labor market. A healthy supply of labor is essential for most organizations. To succeed, businesses, hospitals, schools, and other types of organizations tap into the labor market to recruit the best talent possible. Labor markets do not, however, function in a vacuum. Much like everything else in the economy, they are embedded in society (Berg and Kalleberg 2001). Various institutions shape those markets and, as result, how organizations interact with the labor pools around them. Consider, for instance, the fact that labor markets can be very rigid, very flexible, or anything in between. In very rigid ones, workers move with difficulty from one employer to another: firms cannot dismiss workers easily, obstacles make hiring challenging, workers struggle to find job openings, and more. In very flexible labor markets, firms can fire and hire workers with ease, workers have an easy time finding employment, and so on. Institutions such as legal systems (stating how and when workers can be hired or fired, for example), government policies (related to workforce retraining, for instance, or unemployment benefits), and informal processes (such as how employers share information with each other through networks) shape in profound ways the rigidity or flexibility of labor markets.

Institutions, moreover, have a direct impact on the types of skills workers are likely to develop in any given labor market.

For instance, in coordinated economies like Germany, which has a rigid labor market, industrial associations and trade unions help workers develop specific skills through the use of elaborate educational and training systems. Companies then hire those workers to advance their own strategic goals. Indeed, companies define those goals based on the labor market reality around them. Thus, in coordinated economies such as Germany, we are likely to find companies interested in incremental product innovation (IPI) (which typically depends on very specialized skills), while in more liberal market economies (such as the United Kingdom or the United States) we are bound to observe companies investing in radical product innovation (RPI) (which traditionally depends on workers with general and more flexible skills). Recent research on the chemical industry in Europe shows this to be true (Hermann 2008).

At the same time, companies logically try to circumvent the institutional and labor market conditions surrounding them. Thus, as Hermann (2008) showed, biotech firms in Germany that engage in RPI strategies make up for the lack of general skills by engaging in hiring practices from abroad. In 15 of the country's most reputable biotech firms, CEOs were hired from international labor markets. Firms also use improvisational contractual practices for hiring and keeping labor. In the United Kingdom, where flexible labor market institutions are conducive to RPI strategies, firms using IPI strategies develop firm-specific skills in their employees by investing resources on specific training, using pension schemes to encourage workers to develop their long-term careers in one firm, and offering internships to the best graduates in the relevant fields. When widespread and established, these practices become institutions in their own right: they amount to institutional reactions to imperfect institutional labor market realities.

Interestingly, at times governments produce institutional answers to some of the institutional problems that they themselves have helped generate. These answers have implications for organizations. This has been perhaps most visible in socialist countries, where centrally planned economies can generate abrupt changes in production targets and timelines, and the supply chain (Stark

1986). Such uncertainty means that managers can benefit greatly from a very flexible internal workforce – from being able to switch workers around, alter production plans, and so on. Employees, after all, can be allocated to different jobs inside the organization, while their skills can be utilized in multiple ways by working in any given position. Thus, in Hungary in the 1980s for instance, workers were formally permitted by law to create subcontracting units called "enterprise business working partnerships" (*vállati gazdasági munkaközösségek*). These allowed workers to produce goods or services with their firm's equipment during their off hours and to be paid at a higher rate for their work. This translated into greater labor flexibility nationwide to meet production deadlines (and ensured more wage stability for the workers).

Finally, let us examine the question of location for organizations – a topic taken up by some of the most stimulating research at the moment. Where do firms and businesses choose to set up their manufacturing centers, headquarters, service centers, and other units? And what variables drive those choices? Anyone interested in wealth generation, urban poverty and revitalization, and the consequences for communities of corporate relocations should be keenly interested in knowing how firms decide where to set themselves up in physical terms. Labor market factors play a major role, of course. Firms are likely to situate themselves in areas with strong pools of talented individuals. Yet recent research indicates that institutions at the municipal level play an especially important role. Incomplete and ambiguous information makes it very difficult for organizational managers to decipher the advantages and limitations of any given place, evaluate options, and make decisions. How much reliable data do managers have, for instance, about the labor supply in any given area? Or what objections will community residents and town officials have to a firm's proposal to locate itself in any given area? How costly would a new plant be in one town versus another? Uncertainty is a major problem (McDonough 2007, 2010).

Certain institutions help decrease that uncertainty. Some municipal-based mechanisms, such as established and routinized systems of communication among municipal officials and the public, facilitate interaction and feedback between firms and community residents. On the other hand, some institutions may also aggravate uncertainty surrounding information. Regulations may require organizational managers to go about obtaining information and making decisions in certain specified ways. When these regulations are unclear, information gathering can be extremely difficult.

Field-level institutions

As nearly every college student in the United States knows, US News and World Report (USNWR) – through its magazine and website – publishes enormously influential rankings of colleges and graduate programs each year. The staff at USNWR relies on a set of carefully calibrated, publicly available criteria (for instance, colleges' acceptance rates) to generate their rankings. Virtually no college or university in the United States can afford to ignore the results: if students and their parents pay close attention to them, so should they. Many schools therefore carefully examine the criteria for ranking and then devise ways of improving their performance in one or several of those criteria. A recent study of law schools thus showed that many changed their allocation of resources and altered their admission procedures (to revolve more around Law School Admission Test scores) to score better on the rankings. Some even manipulated data – without actually changing much on the ground – to the same end (Espeland and Sauder 2007).

Taken together, the rankings and their associated criteria contribute to the making of dominant models (for undergraduate programs, law schools, medical schools, and so on) in the field of higher education. Other actors – such as newspapers reporting on the latest rankings, high-school counselors advising students, and agencies offering preparatory programs for entrance exams – play a role as well. Great colleges and universities are those that come at the top of the rankings; poor ones are found at the bottom. The impartiality and objectivity of the ranking criteria are doubted by only a few. The fact that they are "constructed" by observers, experts, arbiters, and others, and therefore subject to political, cultural, and other influences appears to matter little (Sauder and Fine 2008). The fact that they may not be indicators of a college or graduate school's ability to educate students, or that their relevance may vary over time, also matters little. Once a general agreement is in place about the essential characteristics of excellence, alternative interpretations will be few and unpopular. The consensus will prove sticky.

The above example points to dynamics that happen in virtually every organizational field. We can describe them in a more abstract and general form. An organizational field can be likened to an industry, or to a group of organizations which produce similar goods and services. Consumers, suppliers, regulatory agencies, competitors, and sources of funding are also part of these fields (Scott 2008a). We may define an organizational field as the collectivity of all groups and players associated with particular services and products. In organizational fields, there exist dominant models for the sort of activities and processes that organizations should engage in as they try to achieve their objectives. These models are at times as dominant as models found at the global level. Often times, they are more dominant. A number of field-level actors (industry associations, watchdogs, think-tanks, etc.) and practices (such as ranking and rating systems) influence the articulation of those models and pressure players to conform. The USNWR, with its rankings of colleges, offers an example. The activities of the Institute of Nuclear Power Operations offer another example. The institute was set up in 1979 in response to perceptions that ineffective state regulations had been responsible for the partial meltdown of the Three Mile Island nuclear power plant in Harrisburg, Pennsylvania (Campbell 1989). Taking the responsibility of regulation on its own shoulders, the institute pressured nuclear utilities to conform to its own standards, released data and reports about utilities to insurers such that those utilities that did not meet the institute's standards would find their insurability at risk, and stated that it would report breaches of state regulations to the US Nuclear Regulatory Commission. In order to earn the institute's approval, some utilities made very expensive changes in operating procedures.

As is the case for models operating at the global level, dominant models at the field level often have little to do with actual efficiency. Yet, once established, they grant legitimacy and validity to any organization that adopts them, both of which can be instrumental in gaining access to valuable resources (Fligstein 1991). When banks, for instance, are classified by regulators as unsafe, they may be forced to change their practices (Deephouse 1996). There are certainly instances where dominant models originate out of efficiency considerations. For instance, internal labor rotations in Japanese firms may have been behind the impressive performance of those firms in the 1980s and 1990s. But what worked in Japan in those two decades may not work later in time or elsewhere in the world. Nonetheless, once established as dominant, those models are unlikely to be quickly uprooted or altered. Too much depends on them, data on the objective impact of models is rare and difficult to interpret, and learning in organizational settings takes place slowly. Thus, hospitals, for instance, have organized themselves internally in essentially the same way for over a century despite the fact that so much has changed inside and around them.

The stability of particular models is never permanent, however. Interpretations and reinterpretations of those models cause change. New models replace old ones. In the late nineteenth century in the United States, for instance, the firm was understood to be an economic entity whose mission was to undermine competitors via price competition, cartelization, and monopolization. This changed decades later when the firm was seen primarily as a manufacturing entity, whose goal was to produce goods as independently as possible from competitors or other players. The manufacturing model itself eventually fell out of fashion and priority was given to sales and marketing. The new paradigm entailed market expansion rather than the elimination of competitors, and encouraged new organizational strategies like product differentiation and advertising. More recently, the financial conception has taken hold, shifting the emphasis away from the production of goods to the maximization of short-term profits. The strategies appropriate to this new conception include practices like corporate restructuring and stock repurchasing (Fligstein 2004). As these shifting conceptions show, dominant principles and models that shape organizational actions and processes are liable to change, even if this change only takes place slowly. These conceptions clearly occur on a wide scale, as we saw earlier with the stock repurchasing plans at the national level, but they also arise when models of successful firms diffuse to other organizations both within a field and between fields.

What causes change in dominant models in any given field? Institutional factors certainly play a major role. Public policy especially can promote some models and undermine others. This was the case of anti-trust laws in the United States, which pushed organizations away from seeking cooperation via cartels to pursuing competition management via mergers (Dobbin and Dowd 2000). Not all of the factors involved are necessarily institutional, however: they can also be technological, economic, political, and cultural, and may even undercut institutional determinants at times. For instance, in their study of private liberal arts colleges, Kraatz and Zajac (1996) found that changing student preferences (from humanistic toward economic career goals) and an increasing interest among employers in the labor market for specialized skills have prompted schools to make structural changes by offering trade and vocational routes. These changes have clearly contravened field-level institutionalized beliefs of what liberal arts colleges should look like – specifically, that such colleges are meant to provide interdisciplinary, non-technical training and education. New field-level models can emerge out of complex, non-institutional dynamics.

B. Institutions Inside Organizations

Institutions inside organizations shape in profound ways the actions and processes of those organizations. They affect the type of knowledge and information that circulates internally. They facilitate or inhibit learning, and they help or prevent coordination, exposure to attractive markets, access to essential resources, and much more (Argote et al. 2000; Boland and Tenkasi 1995).

We consider in this section three types of institutions that have received considerable attention from economic sociologists: filtering institutions, norms and codes of conduct for everyday behavior, and myths.

Filtering institutions

A number of institutions filter – that, is, both restrict and guide – the flow of knowledge and information *within* organizations. These can be rather informal: they are the unspoken rules and practices around what type of data should, or should not, be gathered and shared, who should know what and when, how data should be collected and disseminated, and more. They exist throughout organizations – at different levels of their hierarchies and across given units.

Consider the fact, for instance, that inside any organization employees belong to certain occupational groups. Each group has its own priorities and approaches for gathering, interpreting, and storing knowledge and information. Research biologists in a pharmaceutical company, for example, utilize certain databases and search engines for collecting data. They share particular understandings of progress or scientific validity. Public health specialists in the same organization are very likely to subscribe to rather different practices and understandings. These are established approaches. Newcomers are socialized into, and receive instructions from those already in, those communities, either explicitly through specific guidelines or implicitly through observation and participation (Bartunek et al. 2003). Each approach is valuable: it helps individuals in a given organization deal in an orderly fashion with an otherwise chaotic and large body of data, and then categorize, process, and store that data. Yet the differences between approaches can at the same time raise considerable barriers to information and knowledge sharing among those groups. One group could be in possession of data that might be valuable to the other group; however, the first group may simply ignore or treat that data as mildly relevant and fail to share it outside of its boundaries. Different perspectives are sometimes perceived to be threatening to the status quo and thus dismissed to the same effect. Potentially valuable insights, when received, are utilized only if packaged and presented in particular formats.

Consider a recent study of the relationships between hospital-based geneticists and primary-care general practitioners in hospitals in the United Kingdom (Martin et al. 2009). Both often serve the same patients. They value each other's perspectives. The geneticist appreciates the broad knowledge of medicine possessed by the general practitioner, while the latter admires the former's depth of expertise. Yet the two groups have deeply entrenched assumptions about each other's limits. Those assumptions are formed and reinforced during training sessions, consultation practices, recommendations from professional associations, and through other venues. Geneticists, for instance, have gradually become suspicious of general practitioners' increasingly specialized knowledge and abilities, and resist their "encroachment" into their community and field of clinical genetics. This has translated into efforts on the part of geneticists to limit more clearly the times and places when general practitioners are expected to interact with patients, and provide their insights and input. More and more virtual walls have therefore been erected between the two groups, with important implications for what sort of knowledge is shared. Similar observations were reported in a different study of a hospital in the United Kingdom (Bate 2000), and of doctors more generally as they relate to nurses (Currie and Suhomlinova 2006).

Recent work on taken-for-granted procedures and routines at staff meetings in corporate settings also shows how institutional variables can either help or inhibit the flow of information. In some cases, they encourage those not in managerial or executive positions to voice their opinions and offer feedback. In those environments where insights and ideas are welcome and routinely invoked from different levels of the organization, innovation and productivity can improve dramatically (De Long and Fahey 2000). In other cases, however, the established procedures and routines only encourage one-way communications from executive leaders to others in the organization. Employees with insights about on-the-ground work realities do not have the occasion to share their knowledge. In those cases, opportunities for training, investment, and other productive initiatives are missed.

At the same time, formal rules and practices also have a great impact on the flows of knowledge and information inside organizations. For instance, over-reliance on formal organizational definitions may serve as barriers to knowledge transfer. Official definitions of various kinds of work may be taken at face value and adopted without questions, making it difficult for knowledge to be shared between older, more experienced employees and newly recruited ones (Brown and Duguid 1991). Thus, when hiring and training is done primarily on the basis of formal aspects of organizational practice, such as job descriptions, instructional manuals, and training programs, other approaches to informal learning may be phased out or simply obstructed. New employees are unable to tap into their more seasoned colleagues' minds. When hiring and training follow more pragmatic considerations, by contrast, the opposite effects may take place.

If we now consider how organizations gather knowledge and information from the *outside* world and transfer them inside their walls, we see that here, too, formal and informal rules and practices play a major role. We can turn again to the health care sector in the United Kingdom to see examples of this. Government policies (themselves institutions, but operating outside organizations) imposed during the 1990s different performance measurements on hospitals and universities (Currie and Suhomlinova 2006). Hospitals were to be rated on the basis of patient waiting times and waiting lists. For medical schools, by contrast, the Research Assessment Exercise placed a premium on publishing in prestigious academic journals rather than on commitment to clinical work. These policy shifts – themselves indicative of broader political changes – stimulated the developments of new rules and practices inside those organizations for gathering knowledge and information from the outside (including from each other). Hospitals began valuing clinical activity-related data above all, and put into place mechanisms and processes that would ensure the capture of such data from outside their organizational confines. Universities instead grew increasingly indifferent to practical data and focused far more on experimental and other related data. They devised and invested in new ways of monitoring and internalizing valuable insights from the outside. Uninterested in each other's knowledge, both sorts of organizations thus began to dismantle initiatives put into place in the 1960s, 1970s, and 1980s that facilitated broad knowledge exchanges between themselves and the outside world. Each organization became far more selective in what sort of information and knowledge it sought, took in, analyzed, and processed. To be clear, this involved more than establishing barriers and selectively discarding data. It was also about cultivating and valuing certain types of information and knowledge over other types – it was about the active pursuit of certain types of data as superior, useful, and therefore worth gathering and capturing.

Institutions for everyday behavior

Employees who feel they can trust their colleagues are likely to be more willing to share valuable knowledge and information that can help them improve their performance. Likewise, trust between members of different organizations or different branches within an organization facilitates the transfer of knowledge that could result in the diffusion of practices proven to be successful in the past. In addition, trust can facilitate the swift execution of daily tasks, the development of social capital, the promotion of more productive capacities, and the coordination of various organizational activities (Hall 2001; Putnam 1993). Some argue that trust is simply a necessary precondition for superior performance and competitive success (Lane 1998). Where, then, does trust come from?

Institutions can have a major impact on trust (Butler 1999; Zand 1972). Some of these take on the form of norms that dictate or guide how individuals ought to behave toward others. Norms of reciprocity, which involve mutual expectations of exchange, either immediately or at some point in the future, are among the most important ones (Putnam 1993). An employee of an insurance company, for example, may feel unmotivated to share her insights into successful policy sales pitches. Why would she take time away from her own tasks to help someone else? Of course, the company as a whole would benefit from it, but the individual employee sees little value for herself. Company-wide expectations that sharing is safe and useful could change things. These could be set over time through training modules, roundtables designed for lesson learning, newsletters, and more. The employee would see not only that others would welcome and appreciate her advice, but that she, too, could benefit from the system. At the same time, trust-inhibiting institutions could also be put into place and have, therefore, the adverse effect. If bonus money was made available on a competitive basis among sales agents, for example, very quickly those agents would not only start withholding valuable information but also doubt the usefulness of what others may be willing to share.

Norms may also encourage individuals, units in organizations, and even entire organizations to share without the condition of reciprocity, which admittedly relies at least in part on some element of self-interested calculation (Lane 1998: 8–10). In what sociologists call "acts of consideration" (Nugent and Abolafia 2006), for example, one party simply feels compelled to come to the aid of another party. When an employee makes a mistake in a project proposal, another employee who notices the error may move to fix it. The accounting department of a manufacturing firm, upon realizing that the sales and billing department regularly mis-categorizes client information, suggests an alternative categorization scheme. A law firm in a particular practice informs its own competitors of a change in law. Norms embodied in internal policies on teamwork, excellence, and responsibility may be behind all of these actions. But other sorts of norms may also be at work: these are widespread and generally embraced expectations – inside single or multiple organizations – about how one should behave in particular situations, how others are to be seen and treated, and the values and beliefs that a particular set of people supposedly share (Lane 1998). Repeated interactions among individuals in organizations encourage the development of those expectations.

There are then established, formal codes of conduct and contracts that make relationships between members of an organization both clearer and predictable (Kramer and Tyler 1996; Rousseau 1989). Explicit or implicit sanctions may be associated with those codes and contracts. Workers in manufacturing companies, for instance, are expected to be committed to producing and supplying good products (Macaulay 1963). Though not necessarily stated in explicit terms, they are expected to report flaws in the manufacturing process. For their efforts, they are rewarded with wages or a salary. The duties and responsibilities of units across organizations are spelled out in company handbooks or, more frequently, developed over time and tacitly subscribed to by generations of personnel. Thus, in many college settings, academic departments produce yearly reports for divisional deans, even though there exists no written policy requiring this. The existence of these codes and contracts enables organizations to function.

Other institutions shape everyday behavior in organizations as well. Among the most relevant are officially recognized certifications and licenses awarded to individuals and organizations by certification boards and professional associations. These can be especially influential in skill-intensive organizations. Employers, contractors, and human resources officials rely on such symbolic items to determine who can and cannot perform certain tasks: those recognitions function as assurances of competence and reliability (Zucker 1986). Hence, technicians who are going to wash high-rise windows or perform industrial work at oil rigs require official documentation from groups like the Industrial Ropes Access Training Association, informing employers and everyone else that the technicians in question possess the necessary skills for the job. Likewise, Scholastic Assessment Test results and the General Certification of Education inform colleges of students' capabilities. At the same time, certifications and licenses can easily become outdated, poorly monitored, or simply unreliable. After all, they amount to socially constructed processes and practices: they reflect power dynamics, opinions, cultural influences, and much more. This does not mean, however, that they suddenly lose their relevance and disappear. As with many other kinds of institutions, they are often sticky and difficult to replace.

We should note that this less benevolent view of institutions echoes a rich and diverse body of research on the impact of institutions on organizational actions and processes. As early as the

1970s, scholars proposed that organizations are rather anarchic spaces where problems, solutions, and people independently move about and at times meet. They utilized the metaphor of a garbage can (Cohen et al. 1972) to describe what happens in organizations. In the most extreme of instances, there is little that coordinates activities, functions, and outputs. Streams of problems reach the organization as autonomous pools of solutions float around. Problems are matched fairly randomly to solutions. People wander aimlessly with presumed, but not realistic, objectives. If something exists to match problems, solutions, and people, it is rather temporary (Olsen 2001: 193). But in many instances, rules and practices – that is, institutions – help problems, solutions, and people meet one another: they help channel and constrain "this multifarious action, thereby shaping the organization's patterns of choice and problem solving" (Bendor et al. 2001: 171). This does not happen very often in the service of any notion of profitability or efficiency. Instead, convenience, preconceptions of how things should function in organizations, and then habits and inertia prove influential.

Myths

Models exist outside of organizations. Earlier in this chapter, we discussed models at the global and field levels. We said that the dominant ones pressure organizations to engage in very particular types of actions and processes. But models, to become dominant, must somehow be internalized by actors and participants. When they do so, they become "myths": sets of established assumptions that actors inside (and outside) of organizations believe about organizations (Meyer and Rowan 1977; Scott 1983: 14). What should a university look like? Most people in universities believe it should have academic departments, professional administrations, a faculty, and a student body. What should they aim for? They should aim to transform undergraduate students into graduates, train graduate students into professionals, and produce knowledge (Kamens 1977). What should a proper hospital look like? What should its mission be? Most people working in hospitals would say that there should be an emergency room, equipment and highly skilled labor to perform diagnoses, tests, and surgeries – all aimed at improving sick or injured people's health.

The internalization of models is both a complex and subtle affair. There is often some resistance and contention, which can translate in outright formal opposition, hidden debate, or anything in between. Some organizational actors (managers or public relations officials, for instance) are more likely than others to embrace (and advance) myths inside organizations. In some organizational fields, the adoption of myths is more partial than in others – depending, for example, on the level of uncertainty in that field. Myths, moreover, evolve over time, with competing interpretations and viewpoints affecting their direction. As Zelizer showed, for instance, American corporations have traditionally relied on bonuses as the appropriate way to motivate senior-level workers. But the nature of those bonuses has changed over time. They used to take on the form of valuable goods such as watches and turkeys. For decades now, they have become cash. At first, corporate leaders had wide discretion over the awarding of those cash awards: most workers did not expect to receive one. Recently, however, they have become a regular part of workers' overall compensation packages (though their amount can vary). Workers feel entitled to them (Zelizer 1996a: 488). Lastly, formal subscription to myths in no way guarantees actual, on-the-ground compliance (Zucker 1986). In some extreme cases, myths remain just that and have little practical impact on organizational structures and behaviors.

Overall, however, just as is the case for models, conformation to myths improves the chances of success by means other than efficiency. Complying with myths generates legitimacy, and legitimacy attracts personnel and capital, garners the support of constituents, eases access to markets, and reduces the likelihood that others will challenge one's activities (Brown 1998; Ashforth and Gibbs 1990; Meyer and Rowan 1977; Scott and Lyman 1968). Failure to conform, by contrast, puts an organization at risk of being labeled unintelligible, redundant, or negligent. Customer bases may shrink, the market value of the organization may drop, contracts with suppliers may not be renewed, and self-governing privileges may be revoked (Hamilton 2006).

The debacle of Enron – a giant oil corporation – in 2001 showed what can happen to organizations when they fail to conform to myths. Enron was discovered to have overstated its profits and understated its debts over the five preceding years by excluding a number of financial partnerships from its accounting records. Many of the aggressive accounting techniques used throughout time were actually *permissible* under generally accepted accounting principles. The same can be said of Enron's investment practices: its sharing of substantial information about its off-the-books investments with potential investment partners but not with its own shareholders did not necessarily violate securities laws. Moreover, the company's restrictions on employees' freedom to sell company stocks (while senior management could) were also within the limits of the law. Yet, when discovered, all these practices caused one of the largest bankruptcies in American history. Why? Because those practices, even though legal, were not in line with current and widespread myths about what a *proper* corporation should and should not do when reporting on its performance and dealing with employees. Employees, investors, creditors, and clients lost "faith" in Enron. The stock price plummeted, funding ran out, and one of the largest corporations in the United States imploded.

C. Isomorphism

Isomorphism refers to the fact that widespread conformity to certain models and myths produces organizations that look and behave alike (DiMaggio and Powell 1983). We have touched upon this idea on several occasions throughout this chapter. But we have not been very systematic about *how*, exactly, institutions generate isomorphism in the actions and processes of organizations. The literature on this important question is well developed and largely in agreement. To begin, scholars see three types of institutional mechanisms at work: coercive, mimetic, and normative.

Coercive mechanisms impose given models and myths onto

organizations. Here, power differentials and dynamics are clearly at work. Organizations face punitive measures if they refuse to follow dominant prescriptions for their actions and processes, and receive rewards for complying. For instance, when it comes to the environment, laws limit the types and quantities of discharge that factories are allowed to release into sewage. In the case of labor rights, regulations require companies to provide their workers with certified safety equipment that is in line with state-endorsed protocols. Failure to comply can lead to heavy financial fees and even jail time. Demands may also at times be less direct. If organizations wish to continue to receive certain types of benefits (such as tax breaks), they must comply with particular requests. Thus, in Huerta's (2009) study of the Amigos Charter Academy, a school in Northern California, new and innovative strategies that were divergent from institutionalized models of schooling were met with skepticism. When district officials threatened to withdraw funds, school officials let go of their vision and embraced a more traditional educational plan.

Mimetic mechanisms involve much more spontaneity than is the case with coercive ones. They are often at work in environments of uncertainty, in which technologies and processes are not well understood, organizational goals are inconsistent and unclear, and ways of meeting these goals or solving related problems are ambiguous (Scott 2001; Cohen et al. 1979). Faced with such a lack of clarity, organizations turn historically successful organizations into idealized models that must be emulated: successful organizations become institutions in their own right. When the anti-sweatshop movement began in the 1990s, for example, many large corporations felt very unsure about what they had to do to avoid being charged by watchdog organizations with poor human rights practices. Feeling vulnerable, and lacking clear instructions, they opted to mimic those organizations that had already adopted successful labor self-regulation after coming under criticism (Wetterberg 2007). They were not required to shift their approach – they chose to do so in light of ongoing challenges and little clarity. Similar events took place in California and elsewhere during the "dot.com" bubble of the late 1990s and early 2000s. Internet start-ups sprang up quickly everywhere – but their presumed services and products were often unclear. Few, if anyone, understood the rapid changes in computer technology. How should companies set themselves up under those conditions? What should their offices look like? What culture should they promote? Unclear about all of this, managers took their cues from a few, highly successful pioneer companies, such as Google: informality, openness, flexibility, and hard work became de facto organizational requirements.

Normative mechanisms are somewhere in between coercive and mimetic ones. They are non-mandatory norms and prescriptions about the behavior and structure of organizations (Scott 2008a). Individuals are exposed to those norms and prescriptions during their professional training – especially in colleges, business schools, medical schools, and so on (DiMaggio and Powell 1983). When they join organizations, they adhere to them and work hard to ensure that the environment around them complies with them. Still in contact with their peers in other organizations through extensive networks, they hold on to those norms and prescriptions over time. They do so not out of necessity, but out of habit, desire for acceptance, and pressure. For example, in his study of the effect of professionalization and networks on corporate support of non-profit organizations in Minneapolis-St Paul, Galaskiewicz (1985) found that corporate giving officers in close contact with each other shared similar ideas of which charitable organizations are most worthy of receiving donations. No one imposed on those officers such ideas about the ideal charitable organization. Instead, those officers adopted them over time without necessarily being even conscious of them. The result was that those corporations acted very similarly when it came to giving, cultivating relationships with their communities, and building their overall corporate image. A second result, of course, was that their giving exercised a certain degree of coercion on the receiving organizations.

We should now emphasize that isomorphism is both complex and often far short of absolute. Regardless of the mechanisms at work, organizations often in fact have room for interpretation and creativity. Take the pricing of goods, for instance. Discounts, mass orders, and high-quality alternatives are all recognized and widely diffused practices familiar to all businesses, but they are often used in different ways by each individual organization (Pedersen and Dobbin 2006). Likewise, while MBA programs have come to be widely offered in business schools throughout Europe, the flavor of those programs varies from country to country (Leiter 2008). Or consider how multinational corporations operating in one country may find that weak enforcement or poorly developed regulation permits certain practices toward employees that are not deemed acceptable in another country. They may be able, for instance, to avoid paying minimum wages, conforming to maximum-hour workdays, or providing safe and sanitary working conditions for their employees. Similarly, although global norms define the range of available options companies have when faced with trying to cut financial costs, companies that are located in countries with strong labor unions, or that have had unpleasant experiences with labor strikes in the past, may be less predisposed to exercise some options (such as pay cuts) than companies located elsewhere.

In addition, an organization's decision to conform depends, at least in part, on how vulnerable it is to issues of legitimacy. Organizations that produce products or services that are vaguely defined may need to do more to establish their legitimacy compared to those that produce more recognized outputs (Bridges and Nelson 2001). Farms can be judged by the tangible quality of their physical produce. Likewise, schools may be evaluated based on the proportion of their students who graduate. In contrast, other organizations with less tangible and recognized outputs, like non-profit organizations, may need to dedicate a greater proportion of their resources to appear legitimate because their output is not easily gauged and evaluated. Moreover, the closer an organization is to public scrutiny and the more reliant it is on public approval, the more likely it is to be judged based on its meeting institutionalized norms and standards (Edelman 1990).

There is, in turn, the real possibility that isomorphism ultimately only happens in good part at a symbolic level, so that conformity to myths (and models) is formal and superficial. Actual day-to-day activities may depart significantly from formal objectives and structures. This is what has come to be known in organizational theory as "decoupling" (Meyer and Rowan 1977). Organizations conform to expectations for ceremonial reasons. Thus, all have official training manuals and job descriptions, but these are not followed in practice. Practical considerations demand that departures be made. "The decoupling of formal goals and daily practice," observed Kalev et al., "may occur because individuals face information overload, and thus stick to the familiar, or because the old ways of doing things have been imbued with meaning and value over time" (2006: 591–2).

Finally, we should note that competing myths (and models) may exist within a given organizational space for organizations as a whole and even for units within organizations. It is possible, therefore, that any given organization finds itself conforming to more than one model – and that internal tensions and discontinuities abound. Moreover, there may after all be more than one version of any given myth (or model). Stories and accounts about what should ideally happen in an organization spread through journals, consultants, expert networks, books, and other channels. Though these can depart only slightly from the original model, sometimes they set standards of their own (Sahlin-Anderson 1996). Entire fields may structure themselves around them. Those who do not adopt them fail and new entrants almost automatically follow them (Fligstein 2001).

Conclusion

Organizations engage in a great number of actions and processes as they seek to acquire, manage, and distribute resources. Institutions have an enormous impact on those activities and processes: to a good extent, they define their very content and evolution over time. Their reach is considerable. Institutions affect everything from the basic structure of organizations to the way organizations articulate their mission, interact with labor markets, communicate with their customers and other external constituents, and set their day-to-day objectives. Thus, we can say without exaggeration that institutions directly shape the *raison d'être* and *modus operandi* of organizations.

Institutions exist at multiple levels – from world society all the way to specific units within organizations. They are therefore both outside and inside of organizations. They range from dominant models at the global level to hard rules promulgated by international or national bodies, to locally taken-for-granted assumptions about the responsibilities of corporations or individuals therein. Institutions inside organizations are often closely related to those outside. For instance, global models directly shape myths inside organizations, and specific corporate governance structures are set by broader legal mandates.

We noted a tendency among organizations toward isomorphism – toward engaging in similar actions and processes. Organizations, especially those in the same fields, tend to "look" alike. We explained this in institutional terms. Coercive institutional mechanisms, such as the law, force organizations down similar paths. Softer – though no less consequential – institutional mechanisms are also at work. In times of uncertainty, organizational actors, almost instinctively and often without evidence to suggest that this might improve their operations, turn successful organizations into models that must be emulated. In more normal times, organizational actors are socialized into environments where particular normative frameworks for organizational design are embraced. The result is organizational convergence.

All of these observations made it obvious that we should resist the tendency – widely shared by economists – to view the impact of institutions on organizations in terms of efficiency. Certainly, in some instances institutions improve how well employees work, products are made, information flows, and so on. Yet to focus on that misses much of the overall impact of institutions. First, institutions can have effects that actually work against efficiency, such as encouraging inertia, resistance to change, and conformity for legitimacy's sake. And second, at a more fundamental level, institutions ultimately define the very essence and life of organizations. This has little to do with efficiency and much more to do with determining what organizations are all about in the first place.

4

National Economies

In this chapter, we are interested in the impact of institutions on national economies. Our attention will turn to three separate questions. First, we wish to know what drives national economic performance. This means output above all: how much do countries produce? How can we account for the fact that the per capita gross domestic product (GDP) of Finland was over US$40,000 in 2010 and that of Malawi was under US$400? Answering this question will require addressing a related matter: what do countries specialize in and why? For instance, why is the software industry very dynamic in India while the Japanese economy is heavily focused on high-tech electronics and manufacturing?

Second, we want to account for large-scale changes in national economies. Specifically, what can explain periods of extended growth or decline in various countries over time? For instance, though they were poor a few decades ago, South Korea, Chile, and China are now relatively rich countries. Zimbabwe, by contrast, has gone from a somewhat well-off country in Africa to one of the poorest nations in the world. What can account for this? In turn, what can explain the particular ways in which countries move from one economic system to another – especially from socialism to capitalism?

Third, we want to understand how key aspects of national economies have reacted to growing exposure to the international economy. Unemployment, poverty rates, the health and longevity of public and private firms, trade liberalization with the rest of the world, and tax regimes are – along with others – some of the most important dimensions of national economic life. Participation in the international economy has affected all of those dimensions. Do we observe certain trends emerging? Have we seen, for instance, a convergence of performance and policies across countries? Have all countries moved toward privatization in similar ways? If divergence persists, what might explain it?

We will see that institutions have a major impact on national economic life. For many economists, institutions such as law or corporatist practices for industrial coordination, when not detrimental to the economy, are primarily responsible for reducing inefficiencies in markets and for defining the incentive and cost structures in any given national economy (North 1990). Such a perspective often places institutions outside of, and often in a subservient role to, the economy of nation-states: the economy could in principle function without institutions but, in some cases, institutions can help the economy run more smoothly. Institutions, according to this view, play a supporting role for the economy. "The work of the 'invisible hand'," noted two economists recently, "can be accelerated by the introduction of a set of rationally designed formal institutions into a system" (Furubotn and Richter 2005: 30). And because the world is constantly changing, institutions must be made flexible, so as to be "able to adapt swiftly and at low cost to new circumstances" (Furubotn and Richter 2005: 34).

Our approach departs from this interpretation of institutions. Sociologists, along with many political scientists, believe that institutions are not outside of national economies but are, in fact, inside of them – an integral part of their very structure and operating mechanisms. Institutions define the relationships among key economic actors, influence the content of economic policymaking, limit but also generate options, filter and distribute key information, make possible certain activities and not others, encourage investments in some areas and not others, and much more. As such, institutions impact national economies certainly, at times, by improving efficiency but also by defining and guiding economic activity. Institutions also mediate the impact of particular variables

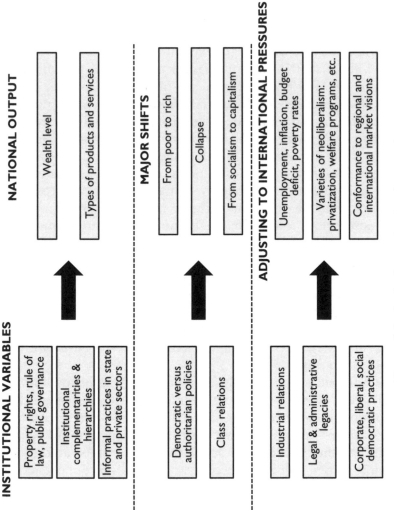

Figure 4.1 Institutions and national economies

on national economies. Thus, one cannot explore the performance of national economies, large-scale changes in national economies, and the relationship between national economies and the international economic environment without considering institutions.

Figure 4.1 identifies some of the most important connections between institutions and national output, large-scale changes, and reactions to international competition. As with the preceding chapters, several key concepts will again inform our discussion throughout. Table 4.1 identifies and defines those concepts. We begin with the question of economic output.

Table 4.1 Key concepts for the economies of nation-states

Key concept	Definition
Institutional competitiveness	Extent to which institutions in a country allow for strong economic performance
Institutional complementarity	Extent to which institutions in a country reinforce each other in their impact on the economy
Path dependence	Economic change seldom brings forth abrupt departures from the past; institutional variables are often responsible for the observed continuity
Neoliberalism	Set of economic policy principles emphasizing privatization, non-state intervention in the economy, competition, and deregulation
Goodness of fit	Degree to which transnational legal principles match existing institutional (law, administrative practices, taken-for-granted assumptions, etc.) realities in a given nation-state

Economic Output

Ensuring on a sustained basis a nation's high economic output has been an explicit objective of political and economic leaders for centuries. Yet there is no simple formula to ensure wealth generation. Too many variables are at work – from cultural to technological, structural, and political. Social scientists in the

1960s, 1970s, and 1980s developed two competing theories for what generates wealth (and wealth disparities) across countries. Neither was institutional at its core, though certainly institutions appeared as important factors in both accounts.

Modernization theory postulated that secularism, scientific mindsets and values, the rule of law, capitalism, and predictability are essential requirements for successful economies. Proponents pointed to Western European countries, the United States, Canada, Australia, and Japan as examples of successfully "modernized" countries. Countries based on more traditional or "backward" cultural, political, and legal systems, by contrast, necessarily exhibited less sophisticated and powerful economies. Those countries were not doomed to failure, however: with competent planning and leadership, they could move up the modernization scale and become like their Western counterparts (Lerner 1964; Inkeles and Smith 1974).

Dependency, along with world-system, theorists also recognized major economic differences among countries throughout the world. For them, however, the arrow of causality did not point to variables internal to any given country, but rather to the nature of the relationship between wealthy and poorer countries (Frank 1969; Chase-Dunn 1989). Certainly, countries struggling economically have weaker or less stable political and legal systems, more unreliability and risk throughout society, more corruption, and other crippling characteristics. Yet this is thought to be a reflection of those countries' position in the broader international economic system and, in particular, vis-à-vis their richer counterparts, which systematically try – via global venues such as the World Bank, military oppression, unfair trade deals, and more – to exploit the former in order to maintain their level of affluence. The nature of capitalism in modern times requires that some countries – usually former colonies of Western powers – operate at the lower end of the economic value chain (producing raw materials and semi-processed goods) and others, mostly the former colonial powers, at the higher end (producing sophisticated finished goods, and offering highly profitable services such as insurance and banking).

Changes in the global economic system from the 1980s onward

undermined both modernization and dependency theories (Inglehart and Baker 2000). The experiences of countries such as South Korea, Chile, Singapore, and China suggested that countries could become successful without necessarily embracing, whole-sale, Western-style "modernity." Multiple paths to economic success were clearly possible. They also made clear that the inter-national economic system was far more flexible than dependency theorists had proposed, since many countries that until recently appeared destined for lower-end production activities started to grow at impressive rates. Observers began to look for alterna-tive explanatory models – less encompassing and grandiose in most instances, but also more precise and testable. A significant amount of attention turned to the role of institutions in produc-ing and supporting a robust and dynamic economic system, and in determining the specific products and services that any given country specializes in. We can now distinguish two types of argu-ments: those stressing the role of discrete sets of institutions, and those emphasizing the relationship – and in particular the level of complementarity – between institutions.

Single institutional factors

A number of distinct institutional variables are important in determining the economic output of any given nation. Institutions present in democratic countries play an especially important role: these include transparent and open elections, checks and balances between branches of government, and recognized and protected individual rights. Countries with these institutions prosper. Those without – such as those ruled by dictatorships (i.e., North Korea and much of Latin America until recently), theocracies (e.g., Iran), nominal democracies (as in Zimbabwe), and other systems of governance – are generally significantly poorer. Table 4.2, which lists the top 20 most successful economies in the world (measured in terms of GDP) for the year 2010, supports such a proposition. Of the top 20, 19 (18 if Russia is excluded) are well-functioning democracies. The only exception seems to be China, but here we must recall that China is at the moment still very much in transition

Table 4.2 National economic output and political systems

Country	Nominal GDP (US$ billions – 2010)	Political system
United States	14,424	Democracy
China	5,745	Socialism
Japan	5,390	Democracy
Germany	3,305	Democracy
France	2,555	Democracy
United Kingdom	2,258	Democracy
Italy	2,036	Democracy
Brazil	2,023	Democracy
Canada	1,563	Democracy
Russia	1,476	Partial democracy
India	1,430	Democracy
Spain	1,374	Democracy
Australia	1,219	Democracy
Mexico	1,004	Democracy
South Korea	986	Democracy
Netherlands	770	Democracy
Turkey	729	Democracy
Indonesia	695	Democracy
Switzerland	522	Democracy
Poland	430	Democracy

Source: International Monetary Fund, World Economic Outlook (October 2010 estimates)

and that, if we control for population size, China is actually still fairly poor (thus, in a sense, China does not really belong to this table but should certainly be taken into consideration when we think about large-scale transitions). The real test for China will be after its economy becomes truly advanced and stable, and whether at that point it can sustain itself without democratic institutions.

If we consider GDP per capita instead as the relevant measurement, the picture does not change much. All but three of the top 20 countries are democracies (with the three non-democratic countries of Qatar, the United Arab Emirates, and Kuwait owing most of their success to oil). If we consider, by contrast, the bottom 20 countries, we find many where functioning democratic institutions are missing, such as Zimbabwe, Afghanistan, Nepal, Malawi, and Timor-Leste. Analyses of particular geographies and time periods confirm this overall trend. Recent research on the continent of Africa, for instance, shows that non-democratic countries have underperformed democratic ones in economic terms (Lewis 2008).

What, exactly, connects democratic institutions to success-ful national economies? Capitalism is especially important. Capitalism is the most productive type of economic system and democratic institutions, with their promotion of individualism, property rights, and freedom, can help capitalism flourish – an insight that certainly echoes some of the postulates of moderniza-tion theory. This general proposition has been followed by more specific claims. According to Jensen, for instance, democratic insti-tutions help attract foreign direct investment (FDI) into countries. As he puts it, "democratic political institutions are associated with higher levels of FDI inflows" (Jensen 2003: 588). Democracies fare especially well in comparison to authoritarian regimes: "demo-cratic governments, even when controlling for other political and economic factors, attract as much as 70% more FDI as a percent-age of GDP than their authoritarian counterparts" (Jensen 2003: 588).

FDI is capital entering a country, not for short-term speculation (as might happen when investors purchase stocks or currencies), but for long-term growth. The targets of FDI are assets such as production equipment, natural resources, real estate, and privately owned companies. FDI can bolster economic output significantly, since it promotes employment, research and development, pro-ductivity, and demand for goods and services. Depending on the industrial base and level of development of a country, FDI can support anything from highly sophisticated industries (such as biotechnology and software design) to raw material extraction and processing. The specific causal mechanism linking democ-racy to FDI is stability: democratic institutions – in particular, the presence of multiple veto-points, checks and balances among branches of government, and the fact that leaders are accountable to the electorate – create fewer risks for foreign investors than non-democratic governments. Those risks include nationalization, expropriations, abrupt changes in taxation regimes, and steep devaluations (Jensen 2003: 594).

Table 4.2 suggests, however, that something other than democracy may also be at work in generating wealth: good governance practices in the public sector. Good governance may be defined as the presence of clear objectives for government agencies and departments, clearly stated rules and roles for officials, effective senior management and oversight mechanisms, sound monitoring practices, and no corruption. Most of these are institutions, and most are generally present in the most successful economies in the world. Their positive impact on the economy is multifold. Investment flocks to countries known to have well-run public sectors. Private-sector players find reliable partners in their counterparts in the state sector: they find them to be good sources of information and guidance. All the while, public-sector agencies and officials can support businesses at various stages in their development and during times of shock. Innovative industries flourish, and established ones endure crises. By contrast, bad governance can hurt national economies in numerous ways. It can generate policies that undermine the business environment, make it very difficult for courts and other entities to resolve business disputes, generate uncertainty, and create uneven grounds for competition. This is indeed the argument put forth by Peter Nicholl, former Deputy Governor of the Reserve Bank of New Zealand (1990–95) and former Governor of the Central Bank of Bosnia and Herzegovina (1997–2004), in his recent reflections on the implications of good and bad public-sector governance for economic performance (Nicholl 2006).

Governance, however, also concerns how governments actively regulate, stimulate, and manage industrial sectors, external trade, and many other aspects of the national economic system. What policies do governments have in place? How do governmental agencies and actors collect, interpret, and then disseminate outside their domains macro and micro economic data? How does the government interface with business and labor? In a recent study of industrial clusters, Borrás and Tsagdis (2008) describe how good governance policies (at the national but also subnational and supranational levels) can encourage very powerful learning, and therefore innovation, among firms in a given national cluster. In China, government subsidies and fiscal policy toward high and clean technologies have done much to stimulate investments and activities in those sectors. Bad policies can have the opposite effect. The global financial crisis of 2008 and 2009 was caused at least in part by risky and aggressive policies in real estate, derivative markets, and lending practices in the United States, Europe, and the international arena – particularly the Basel Committee on Banking Supervision, where representatives from 10 of the most powerful economies in the world meet to agree on capital reserves for banks and other matters. Reforms in the financial sector will hopefully generate more stability and also place certain financial products out of the market while introducing new ones.

State policies on labor markets, in particular, have received considerable attention in recent years. Effective policies keep unemployment levels desirably low and encourage the training and retraining of workers – all things that lead to higher productivity rates for a country. For instance, what happens when, in times of recessions, large amounts of workers are laid off? In some countries, such as Denmark with its "flexicurity" approach, a number of government programs have helped those workers learn new skills and find new jobs (by, among other things, subsidizing training programs or employers willing to hire those workers). Initiatives such as these have proven to be very successful. We should nonetheless note that labor markets are themselves rich with institutional variables – from collective agreements between unions and capital to taken-for-granted assumptions about the responsibilities of unemployed people – and that these matter a great deal for how talent and workers are utilized (Deakin and Sarkar 2008; Deakin 2009), though there is generally significant disagreement amongst experts as to their precise impact. For instance, some researchers have argued that large-scale collective agreements reduce flexibility, mobility, and ultimately productivity. Others have argued the exact opposite, praising instead countries such as Austria and Sweden for their high degree of centralization (Henley and Tsakalotos 1992). At the same time, of course, just about any institution in labor markets is affected in one way or another by government policies and practices. Flexibility, benefits, incentives, rights and responsibilities, training, wages, and much more often depend on national and subnational laws and practices.

Importantly, given the impact of policies on economic performance, scholars have investigated closely the factors that shape the very nature of those policies. Without question, politics and power dynamics between interested actors – such as political parties, labor unions, and business – are obviously of central importance. Yet some of the most critical factors are themselves institutions or are closely related to institutions. In a classic study of taxation policies, Steinmo (1993) showed that electoral rules and practices, and the extent to which political authority is centralized as opposed to fragmented, influence the very content and stability of those policies. Campbell and Hall recently pointed to the presence, especially notable in small and homogenous countries such as Denmark, of "institutional capacities for cooperation, sacrifice, flexible maneuvering, and concerted state action in the national interest" (Campbell and Hall 2009: 547). Radaelli and Schmidt (2005) underscored the role of discourse – understood as sets of ideas and principles made possible by rules about what is admissible, desirable, and consistent with past practice. Schneiberg and Bartley (2001) emphasized the importance of administrative capacity as well as alignment in worldviews among courts and professionals. And Peter Hall, in his analysis of policies in Great Britain and France, described in great detail the impact of "rules, compliance procedures, and standard operating practices that structure the relations between individuals in various units of the polity and the economy" on the direction and content of state policies concerning the economy (Hall 1986: 19).

Some of the most impressive institutionalist research examines the causes of enduring poverty or sub-par economic performance in countries across the world. What can account for the economic struggles of many Latin American nations – a region rich in natural resources and potential but historically unable to match the performance of countries in North America or Europe? Poor policies are certainly in part to blame (Kuczynski and Williamson 2003). Crucially, these include current as well as past policies. Coatsworth argues, for example, that policies set during colonial times have proven highly detrimental to later growth. The reasoning here is that local elites in Latin American colonies were subject to abusive policies set by their imperial masters when it came to trade, monopolistic practices, excise taxes, and much more. The result was that "these hardships imposed on colonial 'elites' were at least as consequential for economic performance as those imposed on the majority populations of the Americas, since most of the colonial population earned too little to invest in the economic future of their societies" (Coatsworth 2008: 557).

Issues with outdated property rights legislation also proved harmful, especially for innovation and entrepreneurial dynamism (Coatsworth 2008: 559). Property rights, in fact, are increasingly at the center of explanations for enduring poverty in Africa and Asia as well. In a revealing study of India, Banerjee and Iyer (2005) found that those rights are crucial for understanding the especially poor performance of some districts. In districts where landlords, rather than cultivators, were given ownership over colonial land, public development expenditure suffered and agricultural investments lagged along with other variables linked to productivity. Legal systems that protect the rights of shareholders of corporations (Mosley and Singer 2008), in turn, positively impact the worth of those corporations. Indeed, property rights in general have been on the minds of sociologists for some time when explaining the performance (output but also dominant types of industries, services, and so on) of economies (Campbell and Lindberg 1990).

But our discussion so far has focused only on formal institutions. Attention should also go to informal institutions, for they, too, are of great consequence for wealth generation. Sometimes, they can have a very positive effect; other times, they can prove detrimental. In Latin America, for instance, informal institutions (such as agreed-upon rules for how to handle foreign-inspired policies and funds) to this date are often misaligned with formal policies and plans, and as such "alter the resulting incentives and related outcomes" in a negative manner (Kingstone 2006: 158).

Thus, we often hear that large amounts of money are misspent or simply go missing. In many cases, informal institutions interact closely with formal policymaking and economic activity, influencing how actors perceive themselves, the world around them, and ultimately decisions about what courses of action are most desirable. This is what Abolafia (2005) showed, for instance, in his incisive analysis of how members of the Federal Open Market Committee – the chief policymaking unit of the US Federal Reserve – arrive at decisions related to interest rates and the purchase or sale of securities. Data has to be interpreted, viewpoints articulated, positions announced and negotiated. Driving all this are taken-for-granted frameworks, procedures, and habits which help the committee members "make sense" of the reality around them and make choices.

And it is what Chibber showed when examining the informal and formal rules and practices shaping how agencies within the state interact with each other and impact the performance of national economies. Do they communicate well with each other? Are their efforts for supporting economic activity well coordinated? The degree to which those agencies, on their own, may appear to be rational and properly functioning is important but not a guarantee that they will successfully support economic actors in the private sector. In the case of India, poor inter-agency relationships have deprived the state of the overall coherency required for developing and then implementing economic development policies. India, as a result, has remained relatively poor when compared to other countries, such as South Korea, where such coordination was put into place (Chibber 2002: 959).

Institutional configurations

Institutions neither exist nor function in isolation. They are inevitably parts of broader environments – cultural, political, legal, and, of special interest to us, institutional. Single institutions relate to other institutions, and this very relationship deserves particular attention. Do sets of institutions in a given national setting influence economic activity there? If so, what exactly is relevant about those institutional sets? What seems to matter most, and with what consequences? In recent years, researchers have made considerable progress in answering these questions.

Some of the most important insights have come from those scholars working within the "varieties of capitalism" paradigm, which itself builds on previous institutional analyses of economies (Amable 2000). First, institutions in any given national economy can *complement* each other. This happens when the presence of one institution increases the returns (for the economy) of another (Hall and Soskice 2001: 17). In advanced, successful capitalist economies, we are likely to observe that institutions in fact do complement each other. This can be the result of pressures stemming from one institution (e.g., corporate governance structures) onto another (e.g., labor market policies). It can also be the outcome of familiarity and reproduction: when certain regulatory principles are known to work well in one area, they may be adopted in another area.

These institutional complementarities shape national economies. In particular, certain configurations stimulate specific types of economic activities and not others. Hall and Soskice observe two major types of institutional arrangements: those associated with liberal market economies (LMEs), and those associated with coordinated market economies (CMEs). The first group includes countries such as Australia, Canada, the United States, and New Zealand. The latter includes countries such as Sweden, Germany, Japan, and Austria. LMEs share a number of complementary institutions: regulatory regimes that are tolerant of mergers and acquisitions, individual-level bargaining between employees and firms, and formal contracts in the private sector to regulate intercompany relations (such as cooperation agreements amongst firms). CMEs also exhibit a number of complementary institutions: access to capital for firms made possible in part by non-publicly available financial data or current returns, complex and collective decision-making procedures and regulations for firm leaders, large-scale bargaining among industry representatives and union leaders, and education and training systems that formally aim at specific and high-level skill acquisition in the labor pool.

These institutional differences between LMEs and CMEs impact national economic activity not so much in terms of quantity of output but rather in the specific kinds of products and services being created. As Hall and Soskice put it, "the institutional structure of a particular economy provides firms with advantages for engaging in specific types of activities there. Firms can perform some types of activities, which allow them to produce some kinds of goods more efficiently than others because of the institutional support they receive for those activities" (Hall and Soskice 2001: 38). In the words of Amable, any given type of institutional configuration gives rise to a "certain pattern of industrial specialization, a certain type of innovation, certain specific characteristics of the labour force in terms of skills or adaptability" (Amable 2000: 657).

In practical terms, we are bound to observe radical technological and product innovation in LMEs. In CMEs, by contrast, innovation tends to be incremental. Radical innovation drives fast-moving technology sectors, such as biotechnology, semiconductors, and software development. It also supports "the provision of complex system-based products, such as telecommunications and defense systems, and their service-sector analogs: airlines, advertising, corporate finance, and entertainment" (Hall and Soskice 2001: 39). Incremental innovation is important for "maintaining competitiveness in the production of capital goods, such as machine tools and factory equipment, consumer durables, engines, and specialized transport equipment" (Hall and Soskice 2001: 39).

There is, therefore, a fair amount of stability and continuity in LMEs and CMEs. The institutional underpinnings of those economic systems support particular types of economic activity. Specific clusters of related industries develop, deepen their reliance on the existing institutional environments, and grow further. Innovations develop within the existing economic systems and generate new technologies and products that advance those industries. All this contrasts, according to Hall and Soskice, with what happens in countries where institutions do not complement each other. There, the harmony we find in LMEs or CMEs is missing.

Economic activity is disjointed, overall output is less, and both the direction and evolution of industries are less clear. In the absence of mutually supporting institutional and economic variables, investments, productivity rates, and growth lag (Hall and Soskice 2001: 45).

Once proposed, the varieties of capitalism paradigm became the subject of significant criticism and refinement. Campbell and Pedersen (2007) put forth some of the most important ideas. They noted that national economies with mixed institutional environments can perform as well as those with more homogeneous environments. Evidence in support of this claim comes from Denmark, which exhibits elements of both an LME and a CME. Such "hybrid" institutional environments may prove successful because different institutions compensate for the shortcomings and deficiencies of others. Denmark's highly flexible labor market (where employers can fire workers with great ease), itself a sign of an LME, could prove damaging for workers, their families, and ultimately the economy. The sophisticated Danish welfare system (with strong unemployment benefits but also retraining programs and job placement support), typical of a CME, however, ensures that those negative effects do not materialize. The combination benefits both capital and labor, and thus Denmark as a whole. In Campbell and Pedersen's view, the variety of capitalism paradigm needs to take "hybrid" institutional systems more seriously. They, too, can be highly competitive (Pedersen 2010). There is probably a rich variety of institutional combinations (besides LMEs and CMEs) that can support successful national economies. And those combinations need not be mapped against the LME-CME model or even against the idea of complementarity, as Amable (2000) and others had shown even before the introduction of the varieties of capitalism paradigm.

There is evidence, moreover, that even in LMEs or CMEs complementarities among institutions are neither as complete (Schneiberg 2007) nor as stable (or self-reinforcing) as proponents of the varieties of capitalism paradigm at first suggested (Hall and Thelen 2009; Crouch 2005). In any given industrial sector, there may be two or more institutional configurations at work, each underlying different viewpoints, traditions, and broader political and cultural developments. This is the case of the soccer industry in Germany and the United Kingdom, for instance, where amateur ideology (according to which the sport should remain tied to local communities, teams should not be seen as engines for profit-making, etc.), on the one hand, and commercialization (that is, increasing reliance on professional managers and players, a focus on money-making, etc.), on the other, have given rise to tensions, opportunities, and changes that point to institutional fractures rather than complementarities (Meier 2008). As such, the system may benefit some actors more than others. Power dynamics must be taken into account to understand how competing institutional logics conflict, mesh, and evolve.

The idea of complementarity, then, offers only one view of how institutions may interact with each other with consequence for economic output. Complementarity implies equality or, at the very least, says little about the possibility that some institutions may dominate others and that the resulting *hierarchy* may make a difference for production modes, innovation, and even the evolution of industries. Amable proposed precisely such an argument: "the hierarchy of institution expresses which part of the institution drives the others, and is helpful for understanding historical evolutions" (Amable 2000: 645). Yet another mode of institutional interaction is *coherence,* or the way in which various institutions in society are in line or are consistent with each other (though they do not necessarily complement or closely function with each other). The list of possible institutions can be quite long. Hollingsworth and Boyer identify the following: "the system of training workers and managers ... the structured relationships among firms in the same industry on the one hand, and on the other firms' relationships with their suppliers and customers ... the conceptions of fairness and justice held by capital and labor ... the structure of the state and its policies; and society's idyosyncratic customs and traditions as well as norms, moral principles, rules, laws, and recipes for action" (Hollingsworth and Boyer 1998: 2). When these institutions are aligned with each other, they push economic activity in some directions and not others.

This was indeed what Hicks and Kenworthy (1998) found as they set out to identify the different kinds of institutional coherency that help key actors in the economy – unions, firms, investors, the state, etc. – cooperate with each other in pursuit of their respective objectives. The authors identified two primary types of institutional alignments (both involving different combinations of formal policies, routines, elaborate rituals, and sets of procedures). The first type promotes tripartite neocorporatist arrangements involving employer associations, union confederations, and states – with the result that national-level agreements are reached on prices, volumes, innovation, and related matters. These institutions are especially in place in the Scandinavian countries, Germany, Austria, and Japan. The second group includes institutions that help firms cooperate with each other without much intervention from the state or other actors. These arrangements make it easier for individual firms to have access to information, investments, and technological advances, with the result that productivity is usually greatly improved in specific industrial sectors. These institutional arrangements are most common in the United Kingdom and its former colonies.

Transitions

National economies are always in a state of flux. Often, this entails minor changes to growth rates, employment patterns, and other economic variables. More rarely, the changes are of a great magnitude and alter in fundamental ways the very nature of those economies. We turn here to two types of transformational changes: major advances or downfalls in national economic growth, and shifts from socialist to capitalist modes of production.

Economic successes and failures

The decades since the end of World War II offer many examples of countries experiencing periods of tremendous economic growth or major downfalls. Instances of success include:

- South Korea: growing at an average of nearly 9 percent a year between 1960 and 1990.
- Chile: growing at around 8 percent yearly for most of the 1990s, and now the country with the highest nominal GDP per capita in South America.
- Ireland: growing at a rate of about 7–8 percent yearly from 1994 to 2001, and continuing to grow thereafter until a major crash in 2008 and 2009.
- China: sustained growth above 7 percent from 1978 to 2010 (except for 1981, 1989, and 1990).

Thailand, Singapore, and Japan offer other examples. Unfortunately, large-scale failures also abound. Among the most recent, Zimbabwe ranks perhaps at the very top. After impressive growth spurts in the 1980s and 1990s, the country's economy contracted by nearly 40 percent during 2000–7, with unemployment rates reaching over 90 percent. Poverty is now widespread, food in short supply, basic services such as education and health care are lacking, and security is very low. A significant number of countries in sub-Saharan Africa also make the list. "Africa's growth performance," an economic historian recently observed, "has been described as the largest economic disaster of the twentieth century" (Aldcroft 2007: 312). Outside of Africa, Nicaragua (GDP per capita annual growth rates between 1970 and 1990 at nearly -4 percent) and other Central American countries turned into economic disaster zones at one point or another. Even highly developed countries have not been immune to massive declines. In Europe, in the wake of the credit crisis of 2008–9, the Icelandic economy simply collapsed. Its stock-market capitalization, for instance, dropped by 90 percent in a matter of a few weeks. While Iceland is likely to recover fast, the same cannot be said of Greece, which was more severely affected by the same crisis.

Such stories of growth and decline require explanation. Many factors are involved, of course. Here, we are interested in the most crucial institutional variables – many of which are likely to differ from those institutional variables that account for given levels (whether high or low) of economic performance in any given country. Change is different from sustained performance, and it is likely to have its own institutional drivers. We consider three institutional sets of variables that drive economic growth, and two sets that are especially responsible for failures.

First, recall the importance of democratic systems of governance for sustained economic performance. There is little doubt that democracy can also fuel rapid economic development. Yet major instances of outstanding growth have taken place under authoritarian regimes, as an impressive statistical analysis of countries across the world between 1950 and 1990 recently showed (Przeworski et al. 2000). "Examples of the purported effectiveness of authoritarian regimes in advancing development," Sáez and Gallagher observed recently, "can be traced to the success of Brazil in the 1930s and 1940s (during the Getúlio Vargas regime), South Korea and Taiwan in the 1960s, and Lee Kuan Yew's Singapore in the 1960s and 1970s. At present, China is portrayed as a notable example" (Sáez and Gallagher 2009: 87). While this may be an uncomfortable claim, and certainly part of a highly conflicted literature on development, the evidence cannot be ignored: it could point to dynamics that, upon closer analysis, may be of relevance for more acceptable kinds of regimes.

Specifically, the primary contribution of authoritarian regimes appears to be the development and upholding (despite protests from other countries and international bodies such as the IMF, the World Bank, and the WTO) of policies aimed at the simultaneous preparation of national industries for competition in the international sectors (especially exports) coupled with their protection (via subsidies, tariffs, quotas, and other instruments) until ready for such competition. East Asia in the 1970s, 1980s, and 1990s offers examples of such "highly successful" policies (Gereffi and Fonda 1992: 434). A second contribution – one that is less likely to be transposable to democratic or other types of regimes – is the related ability of authoritarian regimes to stifle dissent and carry out long-term plans. China, again, offers telling examples: "some would argue," note Sáez and Gallagher, "that China's impressive gains in completing the Three Gorges Dam project and serving as the host of the 2008 Olympic Games is a result of the ability of the state to undertake ambitious developmental projects by quelling opposition and avoiding time-consuming public scrutiny" (Sáez and Gallagher 2009: 88). To all this, even those proposing the benefits of authoritarian regimes are quick to add important caveats. Major periods of growth do not necessarily lead to stable, long-term economic well-being, for instance. Sustainable affluence in most cases requires transitions to democratic regimes. In many authoritarian regimes, moreover, the benefits of growth go to the political and economic elites. South Korea and Singapore may prove exceptions to this, but the Philippines or Malaysia, for instance, support the point.

A second set of institutional variables for increasing success concerns the relationship between firms, the state, and banks. Extensive growth requires access to reliable suppliers, vast amounts of credit, a dynamic private sector capable of innovating, and much more. As it turns out, there is no simple formula for how businesses, the state, and banks should relate to each other. However, we note that certain combinations have proven remarkably successful, with the most compelling evidence coming again from Asia. The economies of Japan, Taiwan, and South Korea posted enormous growth rates in the second half of the twentieth century. If we consider export growth rates alone, the figures are most impressive. Between 1965 and 1984, exports in the three countries grew by 20, 165, and 68 times respectively (Hamilton and Biggart 2001: 446). How did this happen? In a seminal essay, Hamilton and Biggart (2001) argued that economic or cultural approaches alone cannot explain those countries' successes. Attention has to be paid above all to the relationship between the state and businesses, as well as to the relationships among firms within each setting.

Specifically, in South Korea we note the existence of several dozen *chaebols* – large conglomerates of medium to large firms producing complementary goods. *Chaebols* have been at the heart of South Korea's stunning growth. The state not only planned the future direction and activities of the *chaebols,* but also provided direct access to the capital so clearly needed for investment and innovation. This interventionist approach contrasts sharply with what took place in Japan and Taiwan. In Japan, extensive intermarket networks of large firms (e.g., networks of separately owned companies), with their own banks embedded in them, fueled the country's post-World War II recovery. There, the state played the role of mediator above all. Finally, in the case of Taiwan, small, family-owned firms grew at an impressive pace without much state intervention or the presence of closely connected sources of finance. The three approaches, rather than random, were consistent with "time-tested, institutionally acceptable ways" in each country of governing and doing business (Hamilton and Biggart 2001: 464). More recent research has refined and added to precisely this point about institutional continuity. In their analysis of the automotive industries in Argentina, Spain, South Korea, and Taiwan, Biggart and Guillén (1999) emphasize that any given relational configuration among state, business, and other actors must not only be internally coherent but also be in tune with agreed-upon logics of organizational authority and management (Biggart and Guillén 1999).

A third set of institutional variables of importance for economic growth are those promoting long-term political, economic, and social stability. Stability attracts investments, stimulates research and development, and allows for planning, all of which are necessary for genuine advances in productivity. What institutional factors are especially important for ensuring stability? Mechanisms for the peaceful articulation and presentation of preferences, and the resolution of grievances are among the most important. Ireland's stunning growth rates in the 1980s and later is attributed by many, for instance, in part to the Programme for National Recovery, a national agreement on pay and aspects of economic policy agreed to by the government, the Irish Congress of Trade Unions, the Federation of Irish Employers, the Construction Industry Federation, and farming organizations (Fashoyin 2004: 342). The agreement led to controlled inflation, low labor unrest, new job creation, and more. The agreement additionally laid the foundations for the also successful Programme for Economic and Social Progress, Programme for Competitiveness and Work, and Partnership 2000. It was supported by the creation of new councils and organizations for continued social dialogue.

Also important for stability are institutional mechanisms for the redistribution of wealth across social classes (i.e., for material improvements in the livelihoods of those classes, with subsequent improvements in their ability to contribute to the economy). The issue is not without controversy – with some, such as proponents of the so-called Washington Consensus (a shared view among economists and politicians working at the IMF, the World Bank, the United States government, and other entities in Washington, DC, and beyond that favors limited state intervention in the economy, balanced budgets, low trade barriers, and other such measures) and of neoliberalism more generally, believing that growth must come before, and cannot result from, redistribution efforts (Dagdeviren et al. 2002). Those in favor of redistribution argue that the exploitation of large sections of the population – as has happened in many Latin American countries – may generate wealth for small elites but cannot be the basis of a truly dynamic and growing economy. The economic miracles of Japan, Germany, and Italy after World War II offer, by contrast, more positive examples. Those countries were almost completely destroyed by 1945. Yet, by the 1960s, they had become some of the most advanced nations on earth. In Germany, this took the form of well-coordinated corporatism. In Japan, large corporations awarded workers with lifetime employment. And in Italy, it required progressive taxation (in favor of the less wealthy in society) and powerful trade unions able to represent labor. Finally, the success story of nearly every country also points to the importance of sound educational policies in primary and secondary schools. In virtually every Asian case of economic growth, major investments ensured universal access to strong schools for children (World Bank 1993).

What, in turn, accounts for major collapses in national economies? We can differentiate between institutions that shape the interface between a country and the international economic environment, and those that affect the internal functioning of the economy. Failures in either of those types of institutions can have catastrophic consequences for national economies. In many cases, the most critical institutions are policies and regulations (Haggard

1990). Poor governmental policies can destabilize the entire economy of a country in a very short time. Inadequate regulations for the coordination of the activities of state units can undermine investment, reduce information flows, sap foreign investor confidence, increase red-tape costs, and much more (Evans 1995). The results range from sudden jumps in inflation and unemployment rates, to major decreases in credit and export demand. We see both types of variables at work in the cases of Iceland and Zimbabwe.

In the case of Iceland, the policies in question concern the interface between a national economy and the international economic system. Iceland's dramatic growth was fueled by enormous inflows of foreign capital into the country's major banks made possible by aggressive deregulation of the financial sector in the 1990s, in line with neoliberal visions of how financial markets should operate. It was also encouraged by the government's promotion of very high interest rates (around 15 percent). This over-exposure to foreign credit proved lethal as the global financial crisis spread. Foreign investors, worried about the stability of the banks, pulled their money out of Iceland. The result was a rapid depreciation of the Icelandic króna, the related inability of the banks to meet their short-term debt obligations, further panic and withdrawals by foreign creditors, and the virtual freezing of all credit to business. The economy came to a near halt. Iceland's story, importantly, has close parallels in the Baltic countries and Ireland, and it is part of a larger, global crisis precipitated by aggressive and misconstrued financial policies about risk management in countries such as the United States and Great Britain (Campbell 2010a).

The case of Zimbabwe shows something quite different. Poor domestic economic policies – huge fiscal deficits, a corrupt process of land redistribution, the printing of money, and much more – have certainly played a major role in transforming the country's economy from one of the most successful in Africa to one of the worst in the world. But equally important has been the breakdown of internal coordination among, and functioning of, state administrative units, the court system, and the legislative branch. Schools do not function, state officials are not being paid, welfare services are not being delivered, ministries involved with the delivery of health and basic services are at a standstill, and the Reserve Bank has little freedom to act (Brett 2008). Such dysfunction in the institutional make-up of the state has frightened away not only foreign investors but also foreign aid donors, multinational corporations already established in Zimbabwe, and many capable and resourceful national citizens. An internally incoherent state is generally disastrous for a country's economy.

From socialism to capitalism

In 1988, dozens of countries in the world claimed to have socialist economies. By 2010, only a handful could do so. The transition from socialism to capitalism is itself a change from one set of institutions to another: laws about public and private ownership, regulations about the generation and retention of profit, principles of wealth redistribution, the formal recognition of certain personal rights (the right to work, for instance, or inheritance rights), and more. Capitalist markets, like socialist ones, need to be *made* (McNally 2007). For our purposes, we wish to understand better the actual transition from socialism to capitalism. What did that entail? Given that alternative endpoints are possible (i.e., that the structure of firm ownership, size of the firms, fiscal law, notions of private property, and much more can be quite different in any given capitalist system), what can account for the different patterns observable across countries (Russia's oligarchic capitalism, for instance, with its reliance on rapid privatization and raw material exports, as opposed to Poland's dependence on foreign capital, gradual privatization, and the exporting of manufactured goods)? No simple answers to these questions exist. At the same time, it is quite clear that institutional variables have shaped those transitions (Centeno 1994).

By and large, most accounts point to path dependent dynamics (Nee and Cao 1999; Stark 1996; King 2002). Local institutional realities – specifically, pre-existing industrial relations, existing state policies, the internal relationships between state units (including the balance of power between legislative and executive branches), property rights, elite access to resources, and dominant legal traditions – have provided blueprints, tools, cognitive schemas, and ready-made solutions for the transitions. They have also defined and limited the available options. Thus, new patterns of ownership, investment, industrial production and relations, tax codes, governance structures, and banking systems have emerged in the transitioning countries, but most do not represent complete breaks from pre-existing conditions (Bandelj 2008). In China, for instance, we observe the continued heavy involvement of SOEs in defining their own "trajectories of exit" (i.e., how they are to be transformed), and accordingly many governance structures and property rights that are semi-public in nature (Nee and Cao 1999: 803). Differences in the new capitalisms in Poland (and Eastern Europe more generally) versus Russia are, in turn, heavily reflective of existing class structures and established differences in the power and roles of different groups in society (intellectuals, elite bureaucrats, the working class, and more) (King 2002).

At the same time, path dependency is not the only way institutions can affect transitions to capitalism. Consider, for instance, institutions that are endogenous to (i.e., outside of) national economies. Central and Eastern European countries, in their rush to join the EU, offer many telling examples. One of the primary requirements for accession into the EU is the adoption of nearly 100,000 pages of legislation, most of which fall in the sphere of the economy either directly (i.e., product specifications) or indirectly (i.e., environmental regulations). Working closely with the European Commission (the EU's executive body), the new entrants into the EU adopted legislation at different speeds and in different orders. All, however, eventually complied at least formally with the adoption of most laws, though the practical impact surely varied across countries (Glenn 2004). Overall, the new legal system shaped in fundamental ways the sorts of market economies that emerged in those countries (Bandelj 2008: 57). Consider, for instance, EU anti-trust legislation preventing monopolies and cartels in the economy. Articles 81 and 82 of the Treaty of the European Communities (TEC), along with Regulation 4064/89, target price fixing, size of mergers, and preferential treatments.

Before the end of the Cold War, the legislation had a major impact in only two of the "old" EU member-states: the Netherlands (once called "cartel paradise") and Italy (where very large companies had traditionally abused their dominant market positions) (Duina and Oliver 2005). But after 1989, the legislation offered a whole new framework in all of the new member-states from Central and Eastern Europe.

Adapting to the International Economy

National economies operate in global and regional economies. Absolute levels of trade of goods and services across countries (even when adjusted for inflation over time) are at historic highs, and trade levels as a percentage of GDP across the globe have also surpassed the historic highs of the early twentieth century. Since 1960, international exports of merchandise across the world have grown faster than global GDP almost every year (World Trade Organization 2009: chapter 1). Capital moves in and out of national economies faster and in larger quantities than ever before. As the financial crisis of 2008–9 showed, national economies are highly interdependent. A healthy debate exists around the extent to which these figures implicate the entire world economy or certain sections of it – above all North America, Europe, and East Asia (Hirst and Thompson 2009). Figures from RTAs in particular suggest that considerable integration has happened within their confines. A good measure of successful economic integration in an RTA is the increase of one member-state's exports to the other member-states as a percentage of that country's total exports since joining the bloc. During the first 37 years of the EU's existence, member-states showed an average increase of 25 percentage points from the time of entry into the bloc (with the exceptions of Greece and Ireland) (Cameron 1998). In South America, in the first decade of Mercosur's existence, the figure is 33 percentage points (Duina 2006: 20).

Economic globalization, whatever its actual strength and depth, has raised considerable challenges for national economies. The ability of FDI and especially more flexible capital to move in and out of countries with unprecedented ease has made national economies potentially vulnerable to major currency fluctuations, swings in asset prices, and inflation. Governments have felt pressures to deregulate, privatize, cut taxes, liberalize labor markets, cease anti-competitive practices, and more – all of which can have major effects on unemployment levels, poverty rates, training programs, benefit programs for working parents, and much else. As they participate in RTAs, in turn, nation-states have experienced a variety of parallel pressures from above – new transnational laws and regulations, limited capacity for bilateral negotiations with non-RTA countries, new limits on inflation and interest rate targets, and more – with important implications again for key economic actors (labor, for instance), unemployment levels, the evolution of industries, and other dimensions of national economic life.

But pressures do not necessarily translate directly into action and outcomes. Sociologists and others have argued that no direct or simple causal relationships can be drawn between participation in the international economy and the evolution of national economies. They have instead insisted that domestic institutional variables have *mediated* in important ways the impact of international forces at the national level (Campbell 2003; Paul et al. 2003). Distinct economic realities thus continue to exist in different nation-states. We consider these arguments first in light of the global economic marketplace and then with regards to regional integration efforts.

Globalization: mediating institutions

There are good reasons to believe that economic globalization, driven in large part by neoliberal principles (such as the need to lower trade barriers, privatize businesses, and limit state intervention and control over the economy), would push all national economies in a similar direction. Public benefits for the unemployed have come under pressure. Governments have found it harder to coordinate or fund training programs for workers.

Private entities can now manage pensions and other retirement programs. Economic inequalities are increasingly seen as the logical, and acceptable, consequence of international competition. For-profit enterprises promise better results in the management of telecommunications, transportation, and other services previously handled by state entities: "in the last three decades," write two observers, "governments all over the world have privatized state-owned enterprises (SOEs) in all sectors of their economies, including energy, infrastructure, and financial services" (Adams and Mengistu 2008: 78). Governments, in turn, have (because of supposedly lower taxes) fewer resources to spend on stimuli programs, infrastructure, and other areas. All this happens at a time when firms are themselves forced to reduce costs, offer fewer benefits to their employees, and outsource as much as possible to distant countries with lower production and service costs.

Evidence suggests, however, that national economies have responded to pressures stemming from the global economy in rather different fashions. And this has happened, in good part at least, because of the mediating role of institutional variables. For instance, in sub-Saharan Africa, as in much of the developing world, privatization was at first seen by many governments "as a cure for declining economic conditions and large fiscal deficits associated with the poor performance of SOEs" (Adams and Mengistu 2008: 79). Many countries embraced it. Importantly, however, the exact course of privatization (both the quantities of SOEs being privatized as well as the overall prices for which they were sold) varied considerably from country to country. According to Adams and Mengistu (2008), the determining factors were a combination of macroeconomic variables (inflation, for instance) and institutional variables. The institutional variables ranged from the existing regulatory frameworks (how cohesive those frameworks were, for instance), to respect for the law, the extent to which citizens are able to participate in elections, and the independence of the civil service from political interference. In countries where those institutional variables were well developed, privatization proved more likely.

According to a different study, in the case of Chile, Mexico,

Britain, and France, "local institutional conditions and dynamics shaped perceptions of the necessity and purposes of economic liberalization, and the channels through which neoliberal ideas could diffuse and influence policy" (Fourcade-Gourinchas and Babb 2002: 534). The timing, scope, and nature of the transition to neoliberal economies – trade liberalization, deregulation, privatization, and more – thus varied across the four countries. In France and Mexico, the transition was slower and less revolutionary than in Britain and Chile. It also translated into different sets of policies: more focused on integration with the international economy in France and Mexico, more monetarist and inflation-focused in Britain and Chile. A few institutions proved especially critical in shaping these contrasting developments: the existing mechanisms for dealing with social conflicts, and ideological and policy traditions.

If we turn to the newly industrialized countries, such as those in Southeast Asia or Latin America, we see that the deregulation of labor markets certainly took place, along with a weakening of trade unions. Yet the image of the global economy crushing workers and giving firms little choice but to use labor as a dispensable resource with few rights has proven inaccurate. Adjustments had to be made but existing state and industrial policies, the established rules of bargaining, and long-standing assumptions about industrial relations have shaped the actual outcomes. The state – with its policies, approaches, and mechanisms for industrial relations regulation – continues to make a difference. And this has not been against the wishes of business and corporate players. On the contrary, both labor and capital have continued to look at the state as framer and guarantor of agreements (Sil 2003). Indeed, the role of the state as the provider of institutional arrangements that underpin the ability of national economies to perform in the global marketplace for developing and developed countries has been explored and advocated for by a number of observers (Edigheji 1999). For instance, as Sassen put it, "a variety of legislative and judiciary measures executed inside national states" now exist "to ensure guarantees and protection of global capital" (Sassen 1999: 409).

In developing countries, in turn, labor rights have evolved in quite different directions across national contexts. These rights include freedom of association, the right to strike, and collective bargaining. The rise of international corporations and mobile capital puts pressure on labor, but recent research shows that it is ultimately a combination of "domestic interests and institutions that determine" how workers are impacted by those trends (Mosley 2008: 680). Sometimes institutions can counteract the negative pressures put on workers and actually help the latter to capitalize on the positive impact that neoliberalism might have on their rights – for instance, FDI could, in theory, improve labor rights (Mosley and Uno 2007). Among the most influential institutions are the number of veto points in a political system (the higher that number, the less likely that changes in labor rights – whatever those might be – will happen), labor's established links with governing parties, and firms' incentives (via laws and other channels) to retain workers over time. Data suggests that the extent to which labor rights have been historically respected in neighboring countries also makes a difference (Mosley and Uno 2007). There are cases, however, where institutions amplify the negative impact of globalization on workers' rights. Recent research points to Costa Rica as a case in point (Mosley 2008).

Welfare programs have traditionally been the primary instrument for nation-states to support as well as compensate for fluctuations in their economies. Those programs contribute directly to workers' training, health-care access, and unemployment benefits. They help new parents return to work, students attend vocational schools and colleges, physically handicapped people enter the workforce, and immigrants learn their new country's language and customs. They regulate and support pension schemes and retirement accounts. It follows that when we consider the impact of economic globalization on national economies we must ask the following question: how has economic globalization affected national welfare programs? This question is at the very heart of a large number of studies. Most early predictions pointed to a retrenchment of welfare programs, with important and complex implications for unemployment rates, the competitiveness of national industries, investment rates and destinations, and much more (Mosley 2000: 738). Many experts continue to believe this: "common wisdom now suggests," wrote Kus recently, "that in the new international context that favors market solutions to economic problems, the principles of welfare capitalism cannot be sustained" (Kus 2006 489).

Yet such a widespread retrenchment has in fact not happened. "The impact of economic globalisation on the welfare state," noted Kim and Zurlo (2009: 130) recently, "can be neither uniform nor unidirectional." And, as Kus put it, "one might expect to see indisputable evidence of welfare retrenchment across the advanced capitalist world. However, this is not the case" (Kus 2006 489). Most studies account for the resulting continued heterogeneity and size of those programs by pointing to the mediating effects of domestic institutions. Kus, for instance, turns to Britain and France for evidence. In Britain, welfare policies did come under attack, especially in the 1980s. But in France, the state retained its role as supporter and ultimately manager of the economy and its limitations. Why the difference? Kus acknowledges the value of a number of institutional perspectives, such as those emphasizing laws and structures associated with corporatist, liberal, and social democratic states (Swank 2003: Kite 2002), and those pointing to dominant policy discourses in different countries (Schmidt 2001). Yet, in his view, "domestic processes" for making sense of the problems facing national economies and devising solutions were especially important. This is a point consistent with the work of Kim and Zurlo (2009) and their research on welfare regimes – understood to be the combination of existing welfare policies and approaches – and with the arguments put forth by Campbell and Pedersen (2007) in their analysis of Denmark's ability to compete successfully in the era of globalization.

Regional dynamics and institutions

Most countries on earth belong to an RTA. In 1990, there were less than 40 RTAs in existence. Today, there are nearly 200. For the purposes of this chapter, we can define RTAs as spaces where several, usually neighboring, countries decide to merge parts or the whole of their economies. To achieve this goal, they remove some or most tariff and non-tariff barriers to trade so as to liberalize the movement of some combination of goods, capital, services, and labor. Table 4.3 identifies some of the most important RTAs in existence.

Table 4.3 Major RTAs in the world

RTA (start date)	Members	Objectives
EU (1957)	Austria, Belgium, Bulgaria, Cyprus, the Czech Republic, Denmark, Estonia, Finland, France, Germany, Great Britain, Greece, Hungary, Ireland, Italy, Latvia, Lithuania, Luxembourg, Malta, the Netherlands, Poland, Portugal, Romania, Slovakia, Slovenia, Spain, Sweden	Common market: goods, services, capital, and labor with common external tariff
Mercosur (1991)	Argentina, Brazil, Paraguay, Uruguay	Common market: goods, services, capital, and labor with common external tariff
NAFTA (1993) & side agreements on labor and the environment	Canada, Mexico, United States	Free trade area: goods, selected services, all capital, no labor
ASEAN's AFTA (1992) & associated services and investments agreements	Brunei, Burma, Cambodia, Indonesia, Laos, Malaysia, Myanmar, the Philippines, Singapore, Thailand, Vietnam	Free trade area: most goods, most services, and most capital
Andean Community (1969)	Bolivia, Columbia, Ecuador, and Peru	Common market: goods, services, capital, and labor with common external tariff

| COMESA (1994) | Burundi, Comoros, Democratic Republic of Congo, Djibouti, Egypt, Eritrea, Ethiopia, Kenya, Libya, Madagascar, Malawi, Mauritius, Rwanda, Seychelles, Sudan, Swaziland, Uganda, Zambia, Zimbabwe | Common market: goods, services, capital, and labor with common external tariff |
| EFTA (1960) | Iceland, Liechtenstein, Norway, Switzerland | Free trade area: most goods (but for agriculture) and (after 2001) services, capital, and labor |

RTAs can have a major impact on national economies. By lowering barriers to trade with their fellow member-states, countries open their economies to competition from abroad. Both importing and exporting become easier, and decisions made in one member-state have more direct consequences for the other member-states. Such dynamics are in place, of course, in the global economy more generally. Regional integration, however, is typically deeper than global integration (the WTO does not liberalize trade as much as RTAs). The effects of openness are therefore potentially magnified. RTAs, moreover, often come with extensive legal frameworks that the member-states must formally adopt (via ratification or internal adoption of new laws). These can vary in their intensity and scope – but they typically concern a large variety of issue areas such as hundreds, if not thousands, of product certifications, tariff reduction schedules, anti-trust practices, environmental requirements, and worker safety requirements. When incorporated into national systems, these legal frameworks change the nature of national economies: production regimes, cost structures, labor force participation and utilization, types of products being produced (functionalities, quality, etc.), and much more.

The question becomes, then, whether RTAs exercise a direct influence onto national economies or not. The most compelling research to date concerns the EU case (as one of the most advanced types of RTAs) and above all the question of how laws designed to merge national economies are implemented. A rich institutionalist literature on precisely this topic has developed in the last decade or so. We discuss here two of the most important trends.

Historical institutionalists have proposed that the "fit" between domestic institutions and RTA laws determines the extent to which those laws are implemented and, therefore, the degree to which national economies are affected by regional integration. In its original articulation, the fit hypothesis focused on two domestic institutions: policy legacies (understood to be legal traditions and administrative practices) and the organization of interest groups (Duina 1999; Caporaso et al. 2001; Börzel and Risse 2003). If RTA law is in line with those institutions, we can expect it to be incorporated into the national legal system and have an effect on national economies. If it challenges those institutions, legislators and others would resist it and sabotage its implementation.

Thus, for example, legislation of an EU directive (75/117) on equal pay for men and women for work of *equal value* underwent poor implementation in Great Britain because legislators saw it as a departure from established legislation on equal pay for *equal work* only and because of strong opposition by well-organized industrialists against any measures that would raise wages. Women themselves, in turn, could hardly rely on trade unions for representation, since these had been male-dominated for decades. The same directive experienced a very different fate in Italy, by contrast, where it was quickly implemented. There, a long string of collective agreements between trade unions and employers already incorporated the principle of pay for work of equal value. Wage differentials were narrower than elsewhere as a result, and the Italian state could therefore draft legislation that faithfully replicated the EU's requirements (Duina 1999). All this had important implications not only for female workers, but production costs and the competitiveness of firms more generally.

The "goodness of fit" paradigm has appeared to some as being excessively concerned with institutional continuity. Critics have argued that individual actors (politicians, administrators, and so on) and their preferences matter too (Mastenbroek and Kaeding 2006), that links between any given EU law and domestic issues being debated at the moment are important (Falkner et al. 2004), and that national cultures of legal compliance cannot be ignored (Falkner et al. 2005). But they have also suggested that institutional variables other than "fit" may be at work. Among the most important are the veto points in a given national political system. Proponents of this perspective have stressed that different national political systems offer actors different opportunities for approving or rejecting EU law. "Institutional veto points," observed one theorist, "refers to all stages in the decision-making process on which agreement is legally required for a policy change" (Haverland 2000: 83). At those veto points, we find administrators, legislators, committees, pressure groups, technical experts, and more. All provide their input and shape outcomes. Those outcomes may defy any predictions that may be generated in light of the "fit" between EU law and national institutional realities, as a recent analysis of the fate of the EU's packaging waste directive (94/62) (a measure regulating how industrialists and retailers dispose of packaging materials) shows.

In Britain, the implementation of the directive was fast and accurate, despite the fact that the measures imposed significant changes. In Germany, the directive called for relatively minor changes, yet it proved very difficult to implement. Why? In Germany, those opposed to the directive had the opportunity to voice their stance in the *Bundesrat* (the federal council where the 16 states, or *Länders,* meet to discuss legislative matters). This was in line with standard practice of interest representation in the area of environmental regulation and elsewhere: corporatist arrangements in the country have given peak industry associations and other actors access to government structures and officials when it comes to a variety of policy areas. In Britain, by contrast, where government traditionally issues – in the case of the environment but also other areas – semi-voluntary guidelines and engages in informal exchanges with representatives of industry and other sectors of society, those most likely to undermine the implementation process had no strong collective representation and, crucially, "no effective veto point at which [they] could substantially delay the process or modify the outcome of the implementation of the

European Packaging Directive. The institutional structure of the United Kingdom effectively sheltered central government from societal demands. Hence at the end, representatives of leading companies, fearing unilateral action by government, accepted" the EU directive (Haverland 2000: 95).

The impact of RTAs on national economies is a function of more than how RTA law itself is technically implemented, however. Regional integration, once underway, opens national markets to foreign products and producers. Competition is increased, some industries flourish while others suffer, unemployment patterns change, inflows of investment increase in targeted economic sectors, and much more. Many of these changes do not happen in unmediated fashion: institutions shape how they materialize in practice. The elimination of tariffs, for example, is a central element of any RTA. In principle, it leads to an increase in the overall trade of the affected goods. But the specific amounts and direction of that trade, and its implications for firms and workers, very much depend on the domestic policies in place in the member-states, as well as the existing relationships between affected groups and the state. The impact of tariff reduction on corn products in NAFTA offers an excellent illustration of this.

Prior to NAFTA, corn made up 60 percent of cultivated land in Mexico and involved 11 percent of Mexico's laborforce (Nadal 2002: 11). With NAFTA, corn farmers were given 15 years of protection before having to face competition from abroad. In practice, the tariff reduction schedule was accelerated. In less than 10 years, the Mexican corn industry was devastated: cheaper imports from the United States made it impossible for most Mexican farmers to continue production (Duina and Buxbaum 2008: 208–10). The livelihood of entire families – especially already poor, peasant ones – was destroyed. How could this happen, especially when we realize that farmers in the United States have higher costs of production than their Mexican counterparts? If we look at a variety of agricultural products (from soybean to poultry), we see similar outcomes.

The answer lies in a long-established practice by the United States government of subsidizing its farmers. Between 1997 and 2005, experts estimate those subsidies to be nearly US$6.5 billion. American farmers were able to "dump" their corn products in Mexico at prices below cost of production. According to one recent estimate, those subsidies cost Mexican farmers US$13 billion (Wise 2009). Mexican farmers, well aware of these dynamics, organized major protests asking their government to renegotiate tariffs with the United States or take other steps to help them. But those farmers do not enjoy strong access to the government, and the latter has historically favored other sectors of the economy (energy in particular). A succession of Mexican governments has therefore largely ignored their pleas.

Conclusion

Modern nation-states have complex economies. We see variations across countries in output levels and in the types of goods and services being produced. National economies at times undergo major changes – such as extended periods of strong growth, collapse, and transitions from socialism to capitalism. Here, too, we observe important differences across countries – even when we consider only those that grow, for instance, or those that are transitioning to capitalism. Finally, most national economies are exposed to the international economic system – whether at a global or regional level. This presents opportunities but also puts considerable pressures on labor markets, firm performance, underperforming sectors, and many other dimensions of national economic life. Different national economies respond differently to these challenges.

No simple explanatory framework can account for all these outcomes and differences. What is beyond doubt, however, is that institutions play an enormous role in much of what we observe. Those institutions range from the formal (laws, regulations, policies, etc.) to the very informal (widely shared assumptions about how to interpret and make sense of the world, traditions, etc.). They can impact the economy individually or in combination with other institutions (as well as broader political and cultural factors).

They may be found inside the state (regulating, for instance, the relationships among ministries), in the output of governmental activities (policies on inflation, for example, or industrial development), in the private sector (patterns of industrial relations, for instance), or in the public sphere (shared assumptions about the rights and responsibilities of unemployed people, for example).

We should not think of institutions, therefore, as being outside of national economic life or serving as facilitators of exchanges and activities that would otherwise naturally happen, perhaps slowly, on their own. Institutions are not subservient to economic life. Rather, they are always and inevitably inherent components of that life. National economies simply would not exist without institutions. The task for economic sociologists continues to be, therefore, to explore how, exactly, institutions shape and enable national economic life.

5

International Economy

Consider the clothes you are wearing as you are reading this sentence. They, along with the furniture, food, computer, cell phone, and television – to name a few objects – that surround you in your everyday life are either entirely or partly made in foreign countries. We live in an international marketplace. But this is no accident or a simple reflection of countries' desire to trade with each other. Institutions have supported and shaped the process of market integration when it comes to goods, services, capital, and labor. A pivotal moment came in 1944, when world leaders met at Bretton Woods in the mountains of New Hampshire to set up the IMF and what later became the World Bank and the WTO. What have those organizations done for the international economy? What sorts of principles and policies have they put forth to foster trade and promote stability? Moreover, how have those organizations reacted to mounting criticisms of their actions in the 1980s and 1990s? We consider these questions in the first section of this chapter.

The international economy may be more regional than global. NAFTA, ASEAN, Mercosur, the EU, and dozens of other RTAs have given rise to transnational economies among a select number of typically neighboring countries. RTAs amount to perhaps the most deliberate and planned efforts at creating transnational economies. Those efforts have entailed institutional initiatives: laws, administrative programs, and dispute resolution mechanisms above all. We wish to understand those institutions: in particular, what types of legal systems are in place and how are they different as we move across RTAs? What can account for their most important characteristics and what impact have they had on regional integration? We explore these questions in the second section of this chapter.

In the third section, we turn to the proliferation of industry-specific organizations, such as the IASB and the International Standards Organization (ISO). One of their primary objectives has been the promotion and adoption of industry standards (related to quality, manufacturing procedures, professional qualifications, and more) across national boundaries. Normally non-binding, and therefore considered "soft-law," these standards have nonetheless affected countless aspects of the international economy. How many of these organizations are there? How do they operate? What types of standards, exactly, do they promote? And what sorts of factors determine the extent to which these standards are followed in practice?

Our discussion will reveal the close relationship between institutions and the international economy. As is the case for national markets, international markets require a large number and variety of formal and informal rules and practices in order to function. But in the case of the international economy there is widespread public recognition that the making of that economy is a process or project that requires a significant amount of planning, intervention, and oversight. There is also an understanding that multiple options are available – that a number of different institutions can support international market activity. Accordingly, many players have explicitly and openly engaged (or sought to engage) in the formulation of the rules and practices that make possible and shape international economic activity. A number of key concepts will once again guide our investigation, and table 5.1 identifies them.

The IMF, WTO, and World Bank

According to most metrics, the international economy is larger and more dynamic today than it has ever been (Centeno and

Table 5.1 Key concepts for the international economy

Key concept	Definition
International economy	Trade across countries of goods, capital, services, and labor
Conditionalities	Conditions set out by international financial institutions accompanying their distribution of loans, aid, and grants to countries in need
Soft law	Non-binding or quasi-binding regulations, standards, and rules usually agreed upon at the international level by national governments, industry players, and other actors
Standardization	Elimination of formal and informal differences among national regulatory frameworks, cultural norms and expectations, technical requirements, and more
RTAs	Formal agreements to liberalize trade among typically neighboring countries

Cohen 2010). Trade volumes for goods and services are at unprecedented highs in terms of overall value and as a percentage of GDP. More workers (in total numbers and as a percentage of the workforce) migrate from their home countries than ever before in history. Vast amounts of capital move at dazzling speeds in and out of countries, while FDI continues to increase. The number and reach of multinational corporations continue to expand (Huber and Stephens 2005). Some emphasize that much of this activity has concerned North America, Europe, and East Asia (Hirst and Thompson 2009). This refines, rather than undermines, the idea that we live in an international economy. Others point to the fact that international economic activity slowed during the financial crisis of 2008 and 2009. While this is accurate, most data continues to point to an expansion of international economic activity in 2010 and beyond.

To some, the rise of the global economy appears to have spontaneously or naturally occurred. With important advances in technology especially, firms, consumers, and other economic actors gained exposure to products and opportunities beyond their traditional national boundaries. Trade increased, companies expanded their operations, and investors searched for and found new markets. Such accounts are inaccurate, however. A complex web of regulatory initiatives and policies has supported the evolution and growth of the international economy. And when it comes to the global economy, the IMF, the WTO, and the World Bank have been the most important organizations to provide those regulations and policies (Woods 2006; Chorev and Babb 2009). Let us consider the contribution of each organization in turn.

The IMF

With its 186 member countries and its headquarters in Washington, DC, the IMF has contributed to the internationalization of the economy primarily by stabilizing countries' currency exchange rates and ability to make international payments. This has made it possible for many countries to participate – or continue to participate – in the global economy: stable currencies encourage inflow and export of capital, goods, and services. Crises, by contrast, scare away investors, make foreign exports too expensive, and undermine domestic industries and their ability to produce goods and services. The IMF's primary tool for achieving its goals has been loans: countries in financial trouble can request money from the IMF. Thus, for instance, the IMF was very active during the financial crisis in Southeast Asia in the late 1990s, the 1994 Mexican peso crisis, and the recent credit crisis of 2008 and 2009.

IMF loans, however, have come with important "conditionalities" – and it is here that the IMF's institutional role in shaping the global economy is most clear. Presented for decades with the label of Structural Adjustment Programs (SAPs), and later with different terminology, these conditionalities have imposed on the borrowing countries important restrictions and policy guidelines that are generally in line with neoliberal views of how governments and national economies should function and interface with the international economy (Chorev and Babb 2009). To access IMF money, governments are to commit to running conservative budgets, privatizing various types of services, cutting social services, deregulating industries, and lowering tariffs and non-tariff barriers to the trade of goods, services, and capital (Woods 2006: 1). In the eyes of IMF officials, these steps can greatly reduce the chances that a country runs into economic or currency troubles again. Such policy prescriptions have contributed to the making of a very particular type of international economy: one that is primarily driven by private (as opposed to state) enterprises, capitalist, with major divisions of labor (or specializations) across countries, and bound to generate wealth inequalities across the globe.

Importantly, the IMF's SAPs and conditionalities have come under significant attack over time. The organization's motivations and success rate have been questioned, especially in light of the failures of countries believed to have followed the IMF's prescriptions very closely. Critics have pointed to Argentina in 2001 and Kenya in the late 1990s as examples. More generally, the IMF has been deemed by many to be too uniform and insensitive to the different realities in place in any given country. Politicians, academics, and the public have opposed the IMF's "one glove fits all" approach – one that appears to reflect above all the preferences of the most powerful contributors to the fund, such as the United States. As criticisms reached new levels in the late 1980s and 1990s, the IMF began to change its rhetoric and strategy. First, in 2002, the IMF announced a more flexible approach to the imposition of conditionalities on borrowing countries. Then, in 2009, it further loosened those conditionality requirements with the introduction of the Flexible Credit Line: countries that meet certain requirements at the time of application for loans can have access to IMF funds without having to face a long list of prescriptions for further reform.

Third, as an alternative to issuing top-down, coercive guidelines, the IMF has begun articulating and disseminating governance principles in the public sphere (specifically, "standards" and "codes") that leaders in public institutions, such as governments and central banks, but also private corporations will hopefully consider, understand, and adopt (Best 2010: 195). These principles do not target any country in particular; nor are they associated with any specific funding initiative. They constitute general recommendations in line with the IMF's vision of a stable economic order. The remarks of IMF Managing Director Horst Köhler in 2001 at the IMF/World Bank Conference on International Standards and Codes in Washington, DC, describe the organization's current mindset and institutional direction. They make clear not only the IMF's interest in setting new rules but also the rationale behind it:

> Standards and codes are an important tool for achieving the main objectives of the Fund – namely, to promote sustained growth, which is essential for reducing poverty in member countries, and greater stability in international financial markets. They are an integral part of the Fund's work on crisis prevention. But they are also crucial for our efforts to help member countries strengthen their financial systems and take advantage of the opportunities of global capital markets.
>
> While it is still early in the game, there is already evidence that meeting standards can pay off. For example, countries that have introduced shareholder and creditor rights in line with international standards have developed deeper financial markets and, as a result, have grown faster than those countries where these rights are not protected by regulation. In countries where minority shareholder rights were protected, stock markets generally declined less during the recent emerging markets crises. In addition, it is fairly clear that countries like Argentina and Chile were better placed to resist contagion during the Asian crisis because they were known to have systems of banking supervision and capital adequacy that meet or exceed the Basel standards. (Köhler 2001)

Among the most important initiatives of the IMF in the recent past has been the development and endorsement (in collaboration with the World Bank, the Basel Committee on Banking Supervision, and other bodies) of internationally recognized standards and codes in 12 areas. These areas include data, fiscal transparency, and monetary and financial policy transparency. Inevitably, these are very specific sorts of standards and codes – more in line with existing practices in developed countries rather than developing ones. They promote openness, checks and balances, and shared oversight. Again, they are capitalist in nature and aim at restraining government intrusion in the economy. As an example, here are some of the standards and rules laid out in the 2007 Code of Good Practices on Fiscal Transparency:

1. The government sector should be distinguished from the rest of the public sector and from the rest of the economy, and policy and management roles within the public sector should be clear and publicly disclosed.
2. There should be a clear and open legal, regulatory, and administrative framework for fiscal management.
3. Budget preparation should follow an established timetable and be guided by well-defined macroeconomic and fiscal policy objectives.
4. Fiscal information should be presented in a way that facilitates policy analysis and promotes accountability.
5. Fiscal activities should be subject to effective internal oversight and safeguards.

The IMF and the World Bank in turn publish Reports on the Observance of Standards and Codes at the request of member-states to publicize compliance rates and experiences. It is too early to determine the impact of these new standards and codes on the global economy. There is little doubt, however, that they continue to promote a rather conservative and Western – if not neoliberal – view of governance and how countries should behave if they wish to participate successfully in the international economy.

The WTO

The WTO was officially established in 1995. In practice, however, it simply replaced the General Agreement on Tariffs and Trade, which had been in place since 1947. The WTO has 153 members, with another 30 countries acting as observers (which, but for the Vatican, are expected to begin negotiations five years after becoming observers). Located in Geneva, Switzerland, the WTO has directly shaped the international economy by working with its member-states on one critical obstacle to trade: tariff and, from the 1970s on, non-tariff barriers to trade. Most of the attention first went to the trade of goods, with services and investments gaining in importance from the 1980s onwards.

The WTO is a multilateral forum, where combinations of countries (typically developed versus developing ones) negotiate and bargain (Odell 2006). As a result of WTO negotiations and agreements, tariffs have been lowered over the decades by considerable amounts. In the 1950 Torquay (England) round, for instance, countries agreed to a 25 percent reduction in tariffs. In the Uruguay Round – which lasted from 1986 to 1994 – countries agreed to about 40 percent reductions in tariffs, reductions in agricultural subsidies, and full access to textile and clothing from developing countries. The current Doha (Quatar) Round, started in 2001, aims at further reductions in tariffs and non-tariff measures, agreements over labor standards, competition, investments, and more. Due to intense disagreements between developing and developed countries about agriculture, industrial tariffs, and other sensitive topics, the Doha Round is in danger of failing. The year 2008 was an especially trying one, with the biggest disagreement involving the United States, India, and China.

Today, the WTO oversees around 60 different agreements (most resulting from the Uruguay Round and totaling around 550 pages) among the member-states. These agreements have the status of international legal texts and the WTO's decisions over disputes are now legally binding. The WTO itself manages disputes among member-states via informal and formal conflict-resolution mechanisms. As of 1994, the Understanding on Rules and Procedures Governing the Settlement of Disputes (and the input of panels, independent experts, several specialized agencies and organizations, and more) has guided the WTO in its handling of disputes.

The WTO, then, has had a direct institutional hand in facilitating the rise of the international economy: because of agreements reached at the WTO, significant tariff and non-tariff barriers to trade have been eliminated. Here are some examples of the rules agreed to during the Uruguay Round. The first concerns services; the second, technical regulation (i.e., non-trade) barriers to trade. Both require the member-states to treat foreign companies and products in no less favorable terms than domestic ones:

With respect to any measure covered by this Agreement, each Member shall accord immediately and unconditionally to services and service suppliers of any other Member treatment no less favourable than that it accords to like services and service suppliers of any other country. (Article II of the General Agreement on Trade in Services)

Members shall ensure that in respect of technical regulations, products imported from the territory of any Member shall be accorded treatment no less favourable than that accorded to like products of national origin and to like products originating in any other country. (Article 2.1 of the Agreement on Technical Barriers to Trade)

As is the case for the IMF, it is fair to characterize the WTO as an organization promoting a capitalist and largely neoliberal view of the international economy (Chorev and Babb 2009), and thus the interests of powerful countries such as the United States, Great Britain, and Germany, and their corporations especially. Its emphasis on tariff and non-tariff reductions, for instance, and not on compensatory mechanisms and principles for poorer countries, indicates a preoccupation with trade liberalization and not fairness, however defined. Critics have also noted that national market size matters a great deal when it comes to bargaining powers, and that powerful countries have therefore been able to impose undesirable agreements on less powerful ones – something that the WTO has repeatedly promised to address.

The World Bank

The World Bank is headquartered in Washington, DC, and has offices in over 100 countries. With 186 member-states, it is made up of two organizations: the International Bank for Reconstruction and Development (IBRD) and the International Development Association (IDA). The IBRD was established at Bretton Woods in 1944; the IDA in 1960 at the request of several member-states. The contribution of the World Bank to the making of the international economy is perhaps less direct than that of the IMF or the WTO. The World Bank's primary objective is to alleviate poverty throughout the world. To that end, the IBRD has targeted middle-income and creditworthy poorer countries, while the IDA has focused on the world's poorest countries.

Overall, the World Bank engages in three main types of activities: providing low-interest loans, interest-free credits, and grants to developing countries for a wide array of purposes that include investments in education, health, public administration, infrastructure, financial and private-sector development, agriculture, and environmental and natural resource management. Thus, while the IMF has focused on currency problems, the World Bank has pursued progress in more tangible and concrete areas. World Bank funds have been used to build roads, bridges, schools, water wells, irrigation systems, and much more. At the same time, the World Bank has been quite similar to the IMF in one crucial respect: during the 1980s and 1990s, the bank approached recipient countries with a mix of neoliberal requests and conditionalities. To qualify for funds, governments had to promise to balance their budgets (and often cut social and health services), privatize many services, deregulate, remove barriers to trade, and take other steps in line with an overall rather conservative and capitalist understanding of national economies and the role of the state.

The World Bank has thus joined the IMF in promoting a particular view of nation-states and their role in the global economy. The IMF and the World Bank "became pillars of a global, neoliberal order" (Chorev and Babb 2009: 460). Indeed, in many cases, the two organizations coordinated their lending efforts. In their view, international trade should happen among capitalist, fiscally conservative, non-protectionist countries that are heavily reliant on the private sector for wealth production. Investments in infrastructure, education, health and other areas should go to those countries that have demonstrated a willingness and ability to manage those investments wisely.

As a result, much like the IMF, the World Bank has come under severe criticisms from non-governmental organizations, think-tanks, intellectuals, political leaders in developing countries, and many others. The bank has been deemed insensitive to the particularities in place in given countries, and has been accused of actually worsening poverty levels in some of the countries it aided

(Vetterlein 2007). Internal studies by World Bank staff themselves have pointed to a very mixed record (Woods 2006: 5–6). For some, all of this seems to be consistent with, and the logical result of, the fact that the United States has exercised enormous influence on the bank's decisions and policies.

In recent years, partly as a response to these criticisms, the World Bank has revised its approach to conditionality. In 2005, officials agreed on a set of new principles that should accompany the disbursement of funds. Three are especially important:

- Ownership: countries receiving funds must have a track record of commitment to reform and clear policy intentions.
- Harmonization: the bank and the recipient government must agree upfront on a coordinated accountability framework.
- Customization: the bank must customize the accountability framework to fit countries' circumstances. (World Bank 2007)

The bank has also paid progressively more attention to the "social" dimension of economic development (Vetterlein 2007). Programs and recommendations are more tailored to the needs, skills, and abilities of actual people. Gender inequality, people with disabilities, migrants, and other hitherto largely ignored segments of the population are to receive more attention. This has represented an important ideological shift, with new implications for the sorts of nation-states that the bank wishes to see active in the global marketplace. It is, however, too early to determine the actual impact of the new programs and initiatives.

Internal Functioning of the IMF, WTO, and World Bank

If the IMF, WTO, and World Bank have generated some of the most important institutional mechanisms underpinning the international economy, it is also the case that another set of institutions has heavily shaped the very functioning of those organizations and even the articulation of their overarching objectives. As one close observer of the IMF and the World Bank put it, "their own rules and habits explain much of why they have presented globalization as a solution to the challenges they have faced in the world economy" (Woods 2006: 3). The internal functioning of these organizations has become a topic of much research in recent years. We can only point to a few key observations here.

In the IMF, one of the most consequential rules is that some member countries enjoy far greater voting rights than others. When considering loans or major policy decisions, the United States' vote counts for 17 percent of the total. This is higher than any other nation. Most countries count for far less. The figure for Bangladesh is 0.25 percent. These inequalities have enormous effects on what the IMF pursues, how it functions, and its evolution over time. They also reflect a simple internal rule established in 1944, primarily by the United States and Great Britain: the weight of a country's vote is almost directly a reflection of that country's monetary contribution to the fund (i.e., its quota). That contribution, in turn, is a function of the relative size of a country's economy. But, crucially, a member country cannot unilaterally decide to increase its quota even if its economy has been growing faster than those of others. Instead, the decision ultimately falls into the hands of the Executive Board (the most recent changes were announced in November 2010), which has historically proven to be slow and very political in its deliberations. There are then less formal but very important institutions that shape the daily functioning of the IMF. These include taken-for-granted assumptions and viewpoints about the need for the IMF to "manage" economic activity. IMF officials believe, in other words, that the economies of nation-states must be monitored and guided in very particular ways. Simply put, the IMF does not adopt a laissez-faire outlook. Where has this tendency come from? Recent research points to Europe – especially continental Europe – as a source of prescriptions and blueprints (Abdelal 2007).

In the WTO, internal rules shape the relative power of different countries, as well as the process by which countries make their preferences known. Negotiations are often protracted over extended periods of time, with both formal and informal regulations dictating what should be discussed when, with whom, and in what order. Issues can be creatively linked to each other at the bargaining table, so that bargains which would otherwise prove impossible to strike can at times be reached – albeit with compromises on both sides. Outcomes reflect these institutional realities (Odell 2006). Interestingly, though each country is assigned one vote, votes have never been cast and all agreements have so far been reached by consensus through negotiations. The bargaining techniques of countries have been the subject of much scrutiny, with some observers noting that the very rules used for bargaining and negotiations were set by wealthy countries in their own favor, though developing countries have often found themselves in a position to extract key concessions on tariff reductions and opt-outs (Chorev and Babb 2009: 467). This, incidentally, along with other internal institutional features of the WTO, has had important consequences for the ability of the WTO to weather more favorably than the IMF the financial crisis of 2008–9, and to enjoy more legitimacy – with implications for its long-term ability to shape the functioning of the global economy (Chorev and Babb 2009).

The internal setup of the World Bank itself has also been highly consequential for its operations and objectives. Similarly to the IMF, it is a hierarchical organization. But its physical presence in over 100 countries necessarily brings about decentralization of power, information, and practices. Its involvement in concrete infrastructural projects in a variety of sectors, in turn, has promoted a rather diverse workforce: economists are certainly prevalent, but sociologists, anthropologists, engineers, and others play important roles as well. Thus, a rich variety of perspectives circulates inside the World Bank. In addition, for both formal and informal reasons, the World Bank has also been more open to outside influence and opinions than the IMF. This accounts at least in part for its recent turn toward the social dimension of development (Vetterlein 2007; Woods 2006: 8).

Regional Trade Agreements

There are nearly 200 RTAs in the world today. Almost every country on earth belongs to one or more. RTAs differ in objectives (as discussed in chapter 4 – see especially table 4.3). Most current RTAs are young, but some are quite old. The Andean Community, for instance, was established in 1969 and the EU in the 1950s. NAFTA and Mercosur, by contrast, were formed in the 1990s. Most, if not all, RTAs reflect to some degree countries' dissatisfactions with slow and limited progress in multilateral forums such as the WTO. RTAs amount perhaps to the most explicit and planned efforts at creating transnational economies. At a particular point in time, national representatives agree on the goal to integrate their economies: to liberalize the movement of a combination of goods, services, capital, and labor. They face a daunting question: how should they go about creating a single marketplace among the member-states?

Inevitably, the officials charged with the creation of an RTA embark on institution building. They recognize that new rules and practices must be put into place if trade across member-states is to increase. We are interested in understanding better these institutional activities, and in particular the following questions:

1. What sorts of institutions have RTA officials built to support the process of market integration? How do they compare across RTAs?
2. What might explain the similarities and differences?
3. Has the practical impact of those institutions on transnational markets fulfilled the vision of RTA officials?

The Institutions of RTAs

RTAs bring together millions of citizens from different nation-states into an integrated marketplace. What does this require? First of all, tariffs must be reduced. Then non-tariff barriers must also be reduced: quotas, subsidies, fiscal incentives, and also differences in regulatory standards (covering anything from the environment to the rights of women in the workplace to product safety specifications). Behind differences in regulatory standards often lie cultural differences – divergent and often deeply held beliefs about fairness, justice, efficiency, what is desirable and what must be avoided, and much more. RTA officials know that tariff, and at least some non-tariff, barriers must be eliminated. How do they tackle this massive task?

The primary tool has been the production of extensive bodies of law. These laws are rich with what we may call "definitional" and "normative" notions (Duina 2006). Definitional notions define the essential characteristics of objects (e.g., tariffs, quotas, pears, computers, toothpaste), activities (e.g., surgery, investing in stocks, purchasing a home), and agents (e.g., insurance companies, truck drivers, doctors) in the world. Usually, this amounts to specifying something fundamental about their constitution (e.g., the ingredients of chocolate, the fabrics in seat belts), appearance (e.g., water is a colorless liquid), function (e.g., reconditioning of airplane engines has the purpose of bringing those engines to a level of performance equal to that of new engines), or steps required for creation or production (e.g., to become doctors, individuals must take courses in biology, nutrition, physiology, and other areas).

Normative notions, by contrast, do not define the characteristics of existing objects, activities, and agents, but rather stipulate what should ideally happen in the integrated marketplace. The focus is thus on desirable outcomes or situations. They will, for example, stipulate that tariffs should reach a certain level, industrialists should never pollute air beyond certain limits, or trucks transporting dangerous substances should not travel at speeds in excess of 60 miles per hour. Although often not explicitly, normative notions tend to ground their claims in notions of justice or fairness. The first type will make claims on the basis of absolute rights and wrongs (sexual assault is wrong); the latter on the basis of comparisons (wealthy people should pay more taxes than poor people).

Shared definitional and normative notions greatly facilitate trade: they eliminate the need for constant re-negotiation among people from different backgrounds over tariff and non-tariff barriers. Consumers throughout the EU, for instance, now agree with farmers and producers that certain items qualify as tomatoes, others as candy, and yet others as honey. When traveling by plane, they agree with airline companies on what air travel entails. And when in a hospital, they share with doctors the understanding that the latter have undergone a certain kind of scientific and medical training and are thus qualified to take action. Some market activities might take place without shared definitional bases, but they are not likely to be sustained for extended periods of time. If buyers and sellers have different conceptions of what is being exchanged, disappointment is bound to emerge. Unmet expectations engender disappointment and the dissolution of relationships.

Importantly, the definitional and normative laws of RTAs extend beyond the sphere of economic life. This process of expansion is inevitable, since the world of economics overlaps with other spheres of social life, as some scholars of the EU have argued for some time (Fligstein and McNichol 1998; Pierson and Leibfried 1995; Ross 1995). The reduction of non-tariff barriers implies, for instance, that industrialists share similar environmental restrictions, and thus subject themselves to similar definitions of "clean air" or "endangered species." Trade of art products requires shared definitions of terms like "artist," "artwork," and "sculpture." On the normative front, regulation of food production standards demands a shared understanding of desired public health objectives. The environment, art, and public health are thus a few of the many areas affected by the laws of common markets.

How extensive, then, are the legal systems of RTAs? How aggressive has the standardization of the world in RTAs been? We can distinguish between three types of approaches. In some RTAs – such as the EU, Mercosur, and the Andean Community – officials have promulgated thousands of laws with definitional and normative content. There are tens of thousands of pages of directives and regulations in the EU. In the case of Mercosur, there exist over 500 decisions and over 1,000 resolutions. In the Andean Community, we see around 700 decisions and 1,200 resolutions. The vast majority of these provide standardizing definitions and normative judgments for countless objects, activities, and actors related to a huge array of goods, services, investments, and labor issues (Duina 2010). More specifically, by one estimate, EU officials promulgated over 17,000 definitional or normative passages in the realms of the environment, economics, and public health alone between 1959 and 2000. The respective number for Mercosur during 1991 and 2000 is nearly 30,000 (Duina 2006).

In a second group of RTAs, the numbers are somewhat more moderate. These include ASEAN and COMESA. ASEAN officials have developed very detailed and harmonized standards for 20 priority product groups, including items such as motors, engines, condoms, and medical rubber gloves. A large number of procedural and safety standards were also developed for the medical and drug industries. The adoption of the *ASEAN Policy Guideline on Standards and Conformance* in 2005 provided further impetus toward harmonization. At the same time, the same officials have followed the principle of mutual recognition in a variety of industries, ranging from electronics to cosmetics. In line with this principle, regulatory differences are actually not harmonized: producers and consumers in the various countries are asked to accept each other's standards. For our purposes, however, such an approach is also institutional in character: it is a form of regulation – though not one that promotes standardization as such.

COMESA officials have adopted a similar approach. The foundational treaty lays the groundwork for the articulation of harmonizing secondary law, but only in certain policy areas, such as economic and social development. In other areas, such as pharmaceuticals and certain aspects of quality standards for all kinds of products, member-states are asked to respect the principle of mutual recognition. This has logically led to standardization in certain policy areas and not others. In 2004, for instance, the member-states agreed to a wide range of standardizing principles in the area of competition (anti-competitive behaviors, mergers and acquisitions, and consumer protection). But in other areas, mutual acceptance of standards and practices is expected. This has been the case for energy.

In a third group of RTAs, we observe significantly fewer regulations aimed at the standardization of the world and much more reliance on the principle of mutual recognition. Consider here the cases of NAFTA and EFTA. As legal texts, NAFTA only has its foundational agreement and two side agreements – the NAALC on labor and the NAAEC on the environment. If we were to examine the content of these agreements for passages that have definitional and normative content, the numbers are quite low. There are less than 300 definitional passages and approximately 600 normative ones (Duina 2006). Most cluster around a few policy areas – such as the national treatment of, and market access to, goods (chapter 3), agricultural products (chapter 7), and government procurements (chapter 10).

EFTA is similar to NAFTA. Its founding 1960 convention is very brief and comes with no additional legal provisions. A few annexes to the original convention add very little by way of harmonization. Revisions to the convention in 2001 and the adoption of several other, short, annexes changed little in terms of the basic approach to regulation. Tariff removal appears as the most important target, and wide use is made of the principle of mutual recognition.

Accounting for Different Regulatory Environments

RTA officials have created different regulatory systems to advance the process of market integration across the member-states. Their three approaches range from heavy standardization to heavy reliance on the principle of mutual recognition. All are institutional in nature and, of course, all three speak of the extent to which market activity cannot be separated from institutional reality. In the case of standardization, the very objects of trade are "constructed" via legal notions. In the case of mutual recognition, the plurality of goods, capital, services, and labor in a given marketplace depends on, and results directly from, the requirement that countries be open to foreign standards.

We should wonder, then, what can account for the three types of regulatory approaches (standardization, mixed, and mutual recognition). Why is it, for instance, that Mercosur officials have produced so many standardizing laws, while their ASEAN counterparts have proven more ambivalent, and NAFTA officials have sought to rely almost entirely on mutual recognition? Economic explanations do not seem very convincing. To state, for instance, that RTA officials adopted the most efficient legal systems given the local political and business realities begs the question – even if we assume the argument to be accurate – of why one type of legal system is more efficient in one geography and not another. Purely political explanations that suggest that those regional legal systems reflect the preferences of the most powerful member-states raises the question of why those actors have those preferences in the first instance.

A more convincing answer focuses instead on institutional continuity, albeit with attention paid to political realities. The inclination to standardize reminds us of the civil law tradition: it amounts to an attempt to codify the world around us, and then to regulate it. The choice for mutual recognition is consistent with the common law tradition: the emphasis is on minimalist a priori regulation in the hope that societal members can carry on, if provided with broad guidelines. Thus, if operating in RTAs where all or the most powerful member states have civil law traditions, RTA officials are inclined to view economic integration as a legal challenge that calls for a legal response. They will talk about the need for "harmonization" of disparate regulatory regimes. And they will accordingly engage in the production of extensive definitional and normative legal principles at the regional level. The choice will not be a matter of too much deliberation or self-reflection.

By contrast, in RTAs where common law is the legislative tradition of all, or the most powerful, member-states, officials understand the problem of worldview misalignment in quite different terms. In their eyes, the problem before them does not require harmonization: differences in national legal traditions can coexist within a single marketplace. The task is therefore to ask market participants to embrace the principle of mutual recognition. They will accordingly craft a non-intrusive legal system at the regional level. Foundational treaties will not mention the problem of harmonization. And when asked about their choices, these officials will recognize that alternative choices were simply not considered. Finally, in RTAs where some member-states have civil law traditions and other, equally important, member-states have common law traditions, a more mixed approach is bound to appear. In some instances, officials opt for harmonization – and thus ask some member-states to compromise on their worldview. In other instances, the opposite approach is taken and other member-states are asked to deviate from established tradition.

Table 5.2 Dominant national traditions and the design of RTAs

		Minimalist	Mixed	Interventionist
Dominant national traditions	Common law	NAFTA EFTA		
	Mixed traditions		ASEAN COMESA	
	Civil law			EU Mercosur Andean Community

If we turn to some of the most important RTAs in the world, we see that the evidence points to a perfect correspondence between national legal traditions and the legal architecture of RTAs (table 5.2). In the EU, Mercosur, and the Andean Community, all of the founding member-states have civil law traditions. If we consider ASEAN and COMESA, we see important countries with common law traditions but also other important countries with civil law traditions. Finally, when we turn to NAFTA and EFTA, we find that at the time of their founding one powerful member state dwarfed others in terms of economic and political power: the United States for NAFTA, the United Kingdom for EFTA. Both countries – along with Canada – have common law traditions. The conclusion is clear: the institutional architecture of RTAs is itself rooted in deeper institutional realities.

Institutions and the Impact of RTAs

Throughout this book we have argued that the contribution of institutions to economic activity often has little to do with efficiency. Instead, institutions shape and make economic activity possible – guiding, defining, limiting it. Our discussion so far of RTAs has been consistent with this view. But not every scholar of RTAs shares this perspective, and their reasoning is worth pointing out. To some – especially political economists embracing the rational choice theory school of thought – RTAs are rational, purposeful tools that have systematically advanced the economic interests of powerful actors.

The foremost exponents of the rationalist perspective include Moravcsik (1998) and Mansfield and Milner (1997). Their arguments typically have a series of assumptions and steps. First, economic growth and technological advancements make foreign markets attractive. This is especially the case for export-driven industries, but also for import-intensive ones, if already reliant on foreign markets (and subject to tariffs and other cost factors). It follows that representatives of the most powerful industrial, service, and agricultural sectors mobilize to pressure politicians to approach leaders of other countries to explore the possibility of integration. These economic actors know quite well what they want and pressure politicians in effective ways. Politicians swing into action and, with a clear understanding of what needs to happen, craft agreements whose consequence is to advance without failure the interests of their domestic economic counterparts. "On not a single major issue," Moravcsik wrote in reference to all major agreements in the history of the EU, "did governments take a position openly opposed by a major peak industrial, financial, or agricultural interest group" (Moravcsik 1998: 475–6). The resulting agreements always lie, in turn, on the "Pareto-frontier," a zone where all decisions "improve welfare for all governments" (Moravcsik 1998: 25) and subject no major player to unexpectedly harmful principles or policies.

Sociologists and others have criticized such an interpretation. As already seen, institutions contribute to the making of international markets. This is not a matter of efficiency. More to the point, however, institutions, once in place, can quite often frustrate the interests of their creators (and thus be seen as actually rather inefficient creations). For one, rule-making systematically reaches issue areas well beyond the original intentions of planners (Fligstein and Mara-Drita 1996). In addition, officials in many RTAs in Africa and Asia appear to have emulated and borrowed specific regulatory frameworks from the EU (as well as dispute-resolution mechanisms) with little concern for practical outcomes for trade (Helfer et al. 2008; Duina 2010). They have instead been moved by concerns with legitimacy and appropriateness. Yet others have shown that given institutional arrangements have had altogether significant unintended outcomes (Pierson 1996; Duina and Buxbaum 2008).

International Industry Organizations

International non-governmental organizations (INGOs) have seen their numbers swell at an astonishing rate since the end of World War II. Their growth has dwarfed even that of international government organizations (IGOs) during that same time period (Feld et al. 1983; Loya and Boli 1999). Initially, when the Union of International Associations, one of the prime sources for data about INGOs, conducted its first compilation of INGOs in 1909, it identified only 200. The number ballooned over time, climbing to 800 in 1930. By the year 1947, more than 90 of such international organizations were being created annually – the majority of which are still active today. As of the late 1990s, the Union of International Associations was in contact with more than 13,000 INGOs. Of these, almost 60 percent were focused on technical and economic matters (Boli and Thomas 1999), and thus in one way or another participated actively in one or more industrial sectors.

It would be impossible to understand international trade and economic activity more generally without taking into consideration these INGOs: one of their primary contributions has, in fact, been the articulation and propagation of standards that manufacturers and service providers across the world are expected to follow. These organizations have functioned as "more or less authoritative transnational bodies employing limited resources to make rules, set standards, propagate principles . . . vis-à-vis states and other actors" (Boli and Thomas 1997: 172). Many observers now refer to them as standard-developing organizations (Mattli and Büthe 2003) or standardization organizations (SOs) (Werle 2001). Important examples include the International Electrotechnical Commission (IEC) and the ISO. Their focus is above all on standards for physical products, though significant attention has also gone to manufacturing and other types of processes, such as the ISO 9000 series of standards (Brunsson and Jacobsson 2000).

Their practical impact has been enormous: in recent decades, millions of export-oriented businesses have adopted the standards put forth by SOs. Aware that customers and clients will seek reassurance of compliance with those standards, companies have invested considerable resources to revise their processes and products. Invariably, they advertise their compliance certification on their marketing materials, websites, and products themselves. Even non-business organizations have aligned themselves with SOs. Government offices, for instance, not only pressure and help domestic businesses to adopt the standards, but themselves internally adopt them – partly as a way of signaling their competence and communicating to outsiders the proficiency of their country as a whole. Thus, for instance, the New Zealand government promotes the use of international financial reporting standards (IFRS) or the International Public Sector Accounting Standards – themselves based on IFRS – not only at the business level, but also at the governmental level, both nationally and internationally (Robb and Newberry 2007). And even non-exporting companies have sought to align themselves with the most relevant international standards. Foreign investors seeking to acquire stocks or portions of a given company can in fact benefit from the transparency and reassurances that come with compliance with internationally known standards. Companies eager to attract foreign capital thus have very strong incentives to follow those standards.

The result of all this, of course, is not only the facilitation of international trade but the very shaping of exactly what products appear and make up the international marketplace. Global standards define the physical make-up, properties, performance, and qualities of those products. They also define what services companies offer and do not offer at the international (as well as national) level. Put in negative terms, those same standards exclude from the marketplace countless products and services that could, in principle, be there. Thus, global standards also affect firms' research and development efforts, marketing strategies, branding, supply-chain decisions, and much more. At the political level, they influence lobbying activities, coordination among producers, and national regulatory frameworks for economic activity.

The impact of SOs is all the more impressive when we recognize that these organizations are not in a position to issue mandatory standards. They simply lack the authority for doing so. Instead, they must present their standards as "soft" rules or law: as norms, principles, and guidelines that industry players and others should, but are not obligated to, follow if interested in selling their products and services internationally as well as nationally (Jacobsson 2006; Karns and Mingst 2004). What, then, makes these standards so powerful and often impossible to ignore? Several factors are at work. SOs claim to have unique sets of technical experts working on these standards (Feld et al. 1983; Jacobsson and Sahlin-Andersson 2006). They therefore enjoy significant authority to generate them. SOs also go to great lengths to present their standards as advanced, cutting-edge, and necessary for remaining competitive (Boli and Thomas 1997). Many outsiders, in turn, view SO experts as providing objective and neutral recommendations that are free from the influence of political decisions or employer interests (Tamm Hallström 2004). Those experts seem to have in mind lofty goals, such as the public interest, and the protection of the environment, health, and safety (Loya and Boli 1999). Finally, and related to the previous factors, government and private-sector players alike recognize that compliance is necessary to appear legitimate and competent.

Having said this, the adoption of international standards is far from being homogeneous across all, or within particular, industries. In the EU, for instance, adoption is more widespread than in the United States (Mattli and Büthe 2003). This seems to be a function, among other things, of the degree to which firms and other actors have historically been exposed to standardizing pressures and, in turn, to the ability over time of more local standardizing bodies to articulate and impose standards on economic actors. Thus, European firms have been exposed for decades to nationwide standards introduced by organizations such as the British Standards Institution or the German Deutsches Institut für Normung, or by European standards established by regional bodies like the European Committee for Standardization or the European Committee for Electrotechnical Standardization. The same cannot be said of the United States. A second, important, driver of adoption is the very content of those standards: their coherency, correspondence with other standards, and relevance (Corbett and Kirsch 2001).

Let us consider now two representative SOs: the ISO and the IASB. Established in 1947, the ISO boasts the most international standards compared to any other organization. The majority of the ISO's members are national standard developing organizations, the largest and most active of which are private associations; states only have a limited indirect role through national standard bodies and, even then, their interference in standardization matters is often resisted by other firms involved in the process. Non-state bodies like industry associations, professionals, and companies are the primary movers in setting the ISO's standards. Further, in order to attain membership in the ISO, prospective members must first be recognized by the ISO to be representative of all of their respective countries' standardizing interests, including not only governments but also consumers, companies, and scientific communities (Loya and Boli 1999).

By the late 1990s, the ISO had published more than 9,000 sets of standards and more than 500,000 documents relating to those standards (Loya and Boli 1999). The ISO covers a number of different industrial sectors, from informational technology to agriculture to construction. Its output has more than doubled in the last 20 years. Today, the ISO, together with the IEC, accounts for about 85 percent of the world's international standards (Mattli and Büthe 2003). One of the most well-known ISO set of standards – first introduced in 1987 – is the ISO 9000 series. It applies to the quality of organizational processes, with the assumption (sometimes heatedly disputed) that comprehensive and well-documented workflows and activities normally result in final products of higher quality (Furusten 2000; Tamm Hallström 2004).

By the mid-1990s, more than 95,000 organizations from over 86 countries had been certified for complying with ISO 9000 standards, and only a few years later the number of certificates issued had risen to more than 200,000 (Tamm Hallström 2004) and was growing at an annual rate of 50,000 to 60,000 (Corbett and Kirsch 2001). Certification has provided firms with assurance and predictability: in a transnational environment of uncertainty, firms are able to rest assured that firms in other countries with whom they are engaged respect certain guidelines and principles (Morgan 2001). The certification reassures customers as well that certain minimum levels of quality have been met (Tamm Hallström 2004). Third parties such as consulting firms and trade journals regularly emphasize the benefits of compliance, which include "higher credit bond ratings, improved customer satisfaction, better stock control, and expanded markets" (Loya and Boli 1999: 182).

A second and important example of ISO standards concerns tobacco and tobacco products. The ISO's technical committee 126 (ISO/TC 126) aims to standardize the "terminology and test methods for unmanufactured tobacco, all types of tobacco products, materials used for manufacturing tobacco products and tobacco smoke including environmental tobacco smoke aspects; specifications and questions of handling, storage, packaging and transport are included as appropriate" (ISO 2010). The list of products targeted by ISO/TC 126 includes cigarettes, cigars, cigarillos, pipe tobacco, and materials used in the manufacturing of tobacco products. The impact of the ISO's initiatives has been significant: entire countries and trade blocs (such as the EU) have incorporated the ISO's standards in their regulation of tobacco products (Bialous and Yach 2001).

Not all SOs are as broad-reaching as the ISO. Some are very specific in their mandate. The IASB offers a good example. The IASB was first started as the International Accounting Standards Committee in 1973 by representatives of a number of national professional accounting bodies. Initially driven by professionals and accounting firms who tried to push their own respective interests and agendas in setting private international standards, the organization was later transformed into the IASB in 2001, with a revised goal of fostering closer links with national standard setters and of reducing the amount of influence held by professional associations in the organization's standardization processes (Botzem and Quack 2006). Now pursuing a largely independent agenda (Gallhofer and Haslam 2007), the IASB aims to establish a single series of accounting standards across the globe. Specifically, the IASB identifies for itself four principal objectives:

- Develop a single set of high quality, understandable, enforceable, and globally accepted IFRS through its standard-setting body, the IASB.
- Promote the use and rigorous application of those standards.
- Take account of the financial reporting needs of emerging economies and small and medium-sized entities.
- Bring about convergence of national accounting standards and IASB standards.

Like the ISO, the IASB has no direct authority to impose its standards. Yet countless firms and business associations have followed its lead. Even governments around the world have made them mandatory in public enterprises (Jacobsson and Sahlin-Anderson 2006). In over 100 countries, businesses (especially publicly traded companies) and other enterprises are either required or permitted to use IASB standards. The range of industries where IASB standards are observed is therefore enormous: the standards, after all, have wide applicability and affect only how companies track and report resources. But in some cases, as needed, the IASB has also issued industry-specific standards. IAS 41 includes, for instance, standards for agriculture (Greuning

2009): accounting practices, the presentation of financial services, and the necessary disclosures that agricultural enterprises must make. Standards apply to breeding, plantations, pisciculture, and more (Lefter and Roman 2007). IAS 26 applies to companies managing retirement benefit plans and asks that these companies should include in their reports a statement of changes in net assets available for benefits, a summary of significant accounting policies, and a description of the plan and any relevant changes that might have been applied to it.

Importantly, the IASB does not act alone but seeks the collaboration of other organizations, such as the International Organization of Securities Commissions, the EU, the Committee on the Global Financial System of the G-10 central banks, and the International Association of Insurance Supervisors (Jacobsson and Sahlin-Anderson 2006; Tamm Hallström 2004). These organizations can approve and effectively promote adoption of IASB standards among their constituents, sometimes to the exclusion of other competing organizations and standards (Botzem and Quack 2006).

Conclusion

International market activity – the movement of goods, services, capital, and labor across national borders – requires the support of formal and informal rules and practices. Products must be defined, principles of exchange agreed upon, barriers to trade removed, and expectations aligned. Objectives must be agreed upon and practically pursued. The international economy does not spontaneously arise, but must instead be made.

The stakes are obviously huge. If we turn to just a single sector – such as agriculture – we see that entire industries in many countries (and therefore millions of people) feel the effects of whatever rules and practices are agreed upon at the international level. Rapid reduction of tariffs without an accompanying lowering of subsidies, for instance, can destroy the livelihoods of farmers in countries whose governments cannot afford to provide help. This is precisely what has happened in Mexico because of NAFTA and the flooding in of cheaper (because heavily subsidized by the government) corn from the United States. And it is exactly what farmers in India, Brazil, and other developing countries fear when facing pressure at the WTO to open their markets to foreign competition from richer countries. The construction of the international economy has therefore become an intensely social and political process. Countless organizations, actors, and groups mobilize to affect outcomes in their favor or, at least, according to their vision of what seems appropriate, more efficient, or simply just.

Today, even when taking into consideration the credit crisis of 2008–9 and its aftermath, we have a fairly stable, capitalist international economic system where significant trade occurs at the global or regional level. Organizations such as the World Bank, the WTO, and the IMF have actively supported and influenced the nature and evolution of that system – promoting largely policies and programs in line with a neoliberal vision and the world. Officials in RTAs such as the EU and NAFTA, in their pursuit of integration, have also been very active devising regulatory frameworks designed to eliminate or reduce tariff and non-tariff barriers to trade. Finally, a large number of international industry associations and organization have been active – both at the global and regional level – in advancing soft law, often in the form of non-binding standards for corporations to adopt in order to ease cross-national transactions. All these activities make it clear that international economic activity does not simply happen. Rather, a rich variety of rules and practices both shapes it and makes it possible.

Part III

Conclusion

6

———

Challenges and Future Research

Individuals, organizations, and countries all engage in economic activity. Most of us operate in increasingly regional and global markets. As we have seen in the preceding chapters, sociologists argue that institutions both enable and shape economic life. From their perspective, economic life simply cannot exist without institutions. Contrary to what most economists believe, institutions are an *inherent* part of economic life. They partly determine our desires as consumers, what is available in the marketplace for us to purchase, and how exchanges unfold. They define the actions and processes of organizations as they seek to acquire, manage, and distribute resources. They heavily influence national production (both the wealth and the specific products that countries generate), the evolution of national economies, and how those economies respond to exposure to the international economy. And they have a direct bearing on the very foundations and overall capitalist character of the international economy. Sometimes, the overall impact of institutions can be described in terms of efficiency. In most instances, however, it has to do with defining, guiding, and setting boundaries around economic life.

Over the last two decades, economic sociologists have explored in good detail all of these ideas. By now, as we have seen, they have produced a significant body of literature – one that affords us a better grasp of the nature of economic life, and the factors that drive and affect its evolution. The field is maturing. In this last chapter, we take some time to think about the limitations of the existing research and exciting new directions for future work. We turn to five sets of issues in particular:

A. Use and overuse of the concept of institution.
B. Relationship between institutions and culture.
C. Empirical issues.
D. Methodological and disciplinary questions.
E. Change and institutions.

Let us consider each set of issues in turn.

A. The Concept of Institution

Thirty years ago, very few sociologists were putting forth explicitly institutionalist arguments for the functioning of the economy. Today, institutionalist theory has become perhaps the most dominant perspective for economic sociologists. While certainly positive, the proliferation of works has not followed a single, cohesive school of thought. This has allowed for a welcome diversity of perspectives, exciting new insights, and investigations into a broad array of issues. It has also created, however, some conceptual confusion – or, at the very least, a rich but also puzzling multiplicity of ideas that requires ordering and clarification. Two issues in particular stand out.

First, institutions at this point refer to so many things in society that the term "institution" risks losing its meaningfulness. In this book, we limited ourselves to a definition of institutions as "formal and informal rules and practices" shaping the economy. But many economic sociologists use broader definitions. For some, organizations (such as the United States government, the United Nations, trade unions, or firms) can be considered institutions (Dobbin 2004b: 7). For others, certain elements of culture (such as trust or basic values) are also institutions (Zhao 2009: 529). Even when we concern ourselves only with our limited definition of institutions, a baffling number of things qualify as institutions: a nod of approval is as much an institution as a company's employee policies or international law on commerce. Indeed, upon closer scrutiny of that definition, the differences between "informal practices" and what perhaps may be something not really institutional in nature, such as culture, is not always easily decipherable.

It seems worthwhile to ask whether more definitional specificity is necessary. One obvious path would be to produce sub-categorizations of institutions, and reflect on each subcategory individually. After all, what might be said of a nod of approval is probably quite different from what can be said of WTO trade agreements. A useful criterion for categorization could be "micro versus macro." Some institutions (though present in much of society) order, inform, or guide the activities of small groups of individuals. This is the case of a handshake, for instance, or of the informal norms for borrowing money shared by illegal immigrant communities in the United States. Other institutions, by contrast, influence the relationship among major business actors, countries, or even international organizations. Bargaining regulations at the WTO, policy frameworks at the World Bank, and the foundational treaties of RTAs such as NAFTA are examples. The chapters in this book have been organized with this categorization in mind and could serve as inspiration for further clarification.

An alternative path might be to differentiate more clearly between formal and informal institutions. The rationale for doing so would be that each type influences (shapes and enables) the economy in a rather distinctive way. If we take organizations as an example, formal institutions (policies, programs, etc.) are in place, in part, to ensure an organization's conformity with expectations so that it appears legitimate (and can therefore gain access to useful resources). The requirements of everyday life, however, and what in practice needs to happen for an organization to function pressure actors in those organizations to develop alternative (and informal) policies and routines (Meyer 1984). Both types of institutions play important, but rather different, roles for the survival of organizations. Since this is likely to be the case for formal and informal institutions at various levels of the economy, further thought should perhaps be given to identifying, differentiating, and investigating separately each type of institution.

The second issue concerns the role of institutions as either independent or dependent variables in the analysis of the economy. In this book, we looked at institutions in their independent function: as variables that in various ways impact economic life. Many economic sociologists, however, view institutions (in the economy) as things that require explanation: what can account, for instance, for the Danish labor market model, known as "flexicurity," which allows for employers to dismiss workers easily but also helps the newly unemployed with funding, training, and placement programs? Or what can explain differences in corporate governance models (shareholder rights, management rights, the role of the board of directors, etc.) across advanced national economies? Or, when it comes to international development, why is the rule of law more solidly in place in some countries than in others? Answers vary, of course. Sometimes, as we discussed on a few occasions in this book, they are institutional in nature. In other cases, they are not.

Regardless, this overall dual preoccupation with institutions (as independent and dependent variables in the economy) can sometimes translate into a dismissal of other possible variables as unimportant. If, when trying to explain the essence of economic activity, we focus on institutions as that which can explain *and* that which requires explanation, the role of politics, interests, and culture, for instance, may be largely ignored. Yet, since economic life is obviously complex, multiple theoretical frameworks are certainly needed to make sense of it all. Thus, a promising "next step" in the institutionalist literature might very well be an effort to delineate the issue areas and conditions under which the institutionalist framework appears especially powerful and when alternative frameworks (or combinations of frameworks) seem more useful.

B. Institutions and Culture

Institutionalist scholars do not define themselves as students of culture. Culture as an explanatory variable for economic life – and other aspects of social life more generally – was central in Max Weber's account of the rise of capitalism. But it quickly lost its pre-eminence for most of the twentieth century in favor of more structural explanations. Indeed, as Liah Greenfeld recently put it, much of sociology (in the early but also late twentieth century and in the first decade of the twenty-first century) can be said to have followed, often times without explicit or even tacit acknowledgment, the insights of Karl Marx above all – not so much his criticism of capitalism, but his belief in objective, external (to the human mind), and almost tangible structures in society, and that human history is above all a succession of material conditions (Marx's approach became accordingly known as "historical materialism"). "The discipline of sociology," Greenfeld wrote in a critical essay, "belongs squarely – however astonishing this is, when one recognizes the full implications of such belonging – within the philosophical tradition of historical materialism . . . [though] the actual instrument of Marx's, as every, paternity was, of course, a swarm of unthinking carriers of his message" (Greenfeld 2006: 177).

As a matter of fact, however, and in line with Greenfeld's viewpoint, culture *does* have a very close relationship to social structures and, therefore, to many institutions. The challenge is to understand with clarity the nature of that relationship. We could perhaps begin by pointing out that "informal rules and practices" might very well be elements of culture. Clifford Geertz, one of the most pre-eminent anthropologists of the twentieth century, once defined culture as something that can "communicate, perpetuate, and develop . . . knowledge about and attitudes toward life" (Geertz 1973: 89). Informal rules and practices do all of this, of course. But so do more formal ones. Corporate policies banning discriminatory behavior inside an organization say something about the leadership's attitude toward such behavior (and at least that of an important segment of society). When international organizations use established quantitative measures (such as GDP or the Human Development Index) to rank the wealth of countries (Wherry 2004), they are communicating, perpetuating, and contributing to the development of collective assumptions about what constitutes progress and well-being.

Conclusion

Thus, at the very least, we can say that institutions embody culture. If so, we face the task of differentiating institutions from culture. One possibility would be to posit that institutions represent or capture in some sort of stable and permanent manner elements of culture. Stability and permanence define institutions. But surely there is more to institutions than this – for they are certainly more than "crystallized" elements of culture. To return to the Danish flexicurity example, it would be accurate to say that it contains elements of Danish culture (a belief, for example, in entrepreneurial freedom but also in the obligations of the collective to look after the individual) but that it is also much more than that. Ideas and values are combined, in a formal way, with each other (i.e., "if you lose your job, the state will do x and y for you") as parts not only of conceptual frameworks but practical state activities and programs as well as workers' obligations. Flexicurity is thus also about guided interventions and processes. A fairly similar point can be said for a totally different type of institution: international legal agreements about trade. Here, surely, we find present elements of culture. But we note that such agreements have a unique sort of formal forcefulness over important subject matters (such as tariff reduction) that is not often found in culture. The same can be said of the imposition of fines or other forms of punishments for breaching contracts.

All this makes it clear that further thought should be given to the way in which, at once, institutions often embody but are also different from culture. How does culture appear in institutions? What do institutions add to culture? Our investigation would have to be done with the economy in mind, of course.

On the other hand, if we assume – as many scholars do – that institutions are quite different from culture, more attention should be paid to how these two variables relate to each other, especially when it comes to their impact on economic life. For instance, if we agree that the economy is embedded in institutional contexts, we should ask where those contexts come from. Are institutions themselves embedded in cultural contexts? When analyzing economic exchanges among individuals (such as, for instance, auctions), Zelizer stresses the importance of "culturally meaningful institutional supports" for the unfolding of those transactions (Zelizer 2005: 36). In his discussion of the market for blood, Healy talks about "morally-weighted" exchange relationships (Healy 1999). Where, then, do institutions come from? Do they emerge out of culture? If, instead, culture and institutions work side by side in shaping economic activity – if they have parallel influence over it – do they interact (reinforce, undermine, etc.) with each other? Put differently, are institutions and culture normally aligned with each other in a given society? And, if misalignment occurs, what happens to the economy when this takes place? All of these questions deserve more careful exploration.

C. Empirical Issues

As with any field of inquiry, economic sociologists have favored certain empirical issues for investigation over others. Those with an institutionalist perspective have not been an exception. We know quite a lot, for instance, about national policymaking, the transition from socialism to capitalism in the post-Cold War era, the general movement of many countries toward neoliberalism, and labor markets. We know less, by contrast, about a number of other important areas. This is especially the case when we consider recent turmoil and changes in the economy at the global and national levels. We consider here three of the most crucial issues that deserve further attention.

We obviously need to understand better the financial crisis of 2008–9. The idea that the ultimate cause was the deregulation of the financial industry may suggest to some that institutions were not at play. Yet deregulation itself is a misleading term. Economic activity never happens in a vacuum, and the purported deregulation of the financial industry was in fact a revision of existing regulatory frameworks (and not the elimination of frameworks). As Campbell recently put it with reference to the United States, "regulatory reforms closely associated with neoliberalism created perverse incentives that contributed significantly to the increased lending in the mortgage market and increased speculation in other financial markets even as such behavior was becoming increasingly risky" (Campbell 2010a: 65). Certain features of the regulatory environment, then, contributed to the making of the crisis. What are needed now are comprehensive investigations of that regulatory environment – what was it? What brought it about? – with evaluations of the proposed regulatory revisions (in the United States by the Obama administration but also in Europe and at the transnational level through entities such as the IMF), and proposals for sound alternatives.

A second, and related, issue worthy of further analysis is the expansion of soft law at the transnational level and, with that, the proliferation of regional or global standards guiding in nonbinding but nevertheless fairly forceful fashion anything from accounting practices at firms to bankruptcy proceedings for companies with operations in multiple countries, to manufacturing processes (and thus the very nature of products we, as consumers, purchase on a daily basis). In the last chapter, we mentioned INGOs as the primary producers of soft law. But international governmental organizations have also contributed directly to the process. In the EU, for instance, member-states have agreed to participate in the Open Method of Coordination, a process whereby, following the guidance of the European Commission especially, shared indicators for measuring economic and social problems (unemployment, for instance) are agreed upon, information on best practices is shared, objectives are collectively decided, and reports on each country's progress are made public and evaluated. In the case of the Asia-Pacific Economic Cooperation, member-states have reached agreements about trade and, since 2001, security and terrorism, that are voluntary in nature but come with strong expectations of compliance. And major bodies such as the United Nations issue declarations and resolutions that, though not mandatory, carry moral weight.

In all of these examples, governments and private actors alike increasingly find themselves following principles and norms, emanating from the transnational but also national levels and quite often not from traditional national legislative processes, which are neither binding nor obligatory. This is a deviation from what has happened for much of the twentieth century. The volume and forcefulness of soft law are growing, and the implications for economic life are enormous, varied, and highly complex. Yet we are only in the early stages of understanding those implications (Djelic and Sahlin-Andresson 2008; Brunsson and Jacobsson 2000). More comparative, theoretically informed, and empirically rich research is needed. We need clearer categorizations of soft law, better understandings of its workings across local, organizational, national, and transnational levels.

A third and pressing issue in need of further attention is the informal economy. In developing countries, the informal economy constitutes a significant portion of the national economy. In developed economies, it is smaller but nonetheless sizeable. Because of this, a variety of social scientists have taken the informal economy seriously for quite some time (Macharia 1997): how does it support the formal economy? Who is in it and why? Under what local, national, and transnational conditions is it likely to emerge? Who controls it? How do transactions unfold and what ensures safety and the fulfillment of obligations? Plenty of case studies speak to these questions. As we saw in chapter 2, for instance, recent comparative work on prostitution in Havana and Amsterdam accounts for differences in those two places by examining institutional variables (such as law) and how they interact with immigration trends, culture, power dynamics, and consumerism (Wonders and Michalowski 2001). A second, well-known, study explored how illegal immigrants in South Florida and New York gain access to loans without formal contract because of several cultural, political, and institutional (the well-known practice by those in the community of ostracizing those who fail to honor their debt obligations) variables (Portes and Sensenbrenner 1993).

Yet what we are still missing are well-developed, explicit *institutionalist* theories and approaches that can improve our understanding of the informal economy and its functioning. Institutions often appear as one of many factors, and clear analytical frameworks for how they relate to the informal economy are generally missing. This certainly needs to change. Especially because of the global economic crisis of 2008–9, the informal economy will grow and develop in new directions, and establish new types of links with the formal economy, as history shows has happened in times of difficulty and crisis (Burroni et al. 2008). An institutionalist analysis of such changes can shed valuable light on these changes. It should certainly be part of the future research agenda of economic sociologists.

D. Methodological and Disciplinary Questions

A quick scan of the literature reveals that economic sociologists rely on very different methodological approaches to investigate the impact of institutions on the economy. Ethnography, surveys, archival work, interpretative analyses, statistical analyses, textual coding, interviews, and other techniques have all been used. This methodological pluralism is certainly welcome, since different questions often require different methodologies to be answered most satisfactorily. Moreover, any given methodology can yield unique insights into a particular economic phenomenon. For instance, if we are interested in grasping the spread of corporate social responsibility policies in North American and European companies, statistical investigations may show, for instance, that forms of ownership (public versus private) may explain why some companies are early adopters; in-depth interviews with company executives may on the other hand reveal the internal logic given for the adoption of those policies.

Or, to go back to our previous discussion, consider the case of the informal economy. Recent institutionalist research suggests that neoliberal policies in Latin America have, contrary to expectations, promoted the expansion of informal economic activities. This has happened, in part, because of multinational companies opening branches in new cities throughout the region, the related arrival of high-salary professionals, and an inevitable rise in demand for services such as gardening, cleaning, and childcare. Poor workers operating in the shadow of the formal economy have proven more than willing to provide those services (Portes and Roberts 2005). Such a causal relationship between broad institutionalist factors, such as international and national policies and the informal economy, can be shown to have taken place with large data sets on cities, companies, job growth, and so on, and sophisticated statistical analysis. But it can also be documented by taking two or three representative case studies and delving deeply, in qualitative fashion, into what has taken place in each instance: which companies expanded, what sorts of professionals appeared on the scene, how locals made sense of the opportunities before them, local laws and industries, the likely conflicts and resolutions created by the change, and so on.

Yet, as research progresses, economic sociologists working with institutionalist theories may benefit from an explicit and detailed overview of each methodology's specific tools, primary advantages and limitations, and the types of empirical puzzles and questions for which each methodology is best suited. Large-scale statistical analyses, for instance, typically show correlations or other sorts of relationships between variables; causality can at times be inferred from these analyses, but it cannot be proven with certainty. Researchers thus need to spell out the hypothesized causal mechanisms. They must also rely on large numbers of observations or case studies. And they obviously should be able to quantify the variables in question. It seems reasonable to suggest that such analyses are most suited for certain kinds of investigations and not others.

In-depth interviews, by contrast, can sometimes be used to probe into those causal mechanisms that statistical analyses cannot properly explore. Because of this, they can at times complement or add to established statistical results. If we know, for instance, that certain types of corporate governance practices appear to be correlated with a high incidence of employee turnover among mid-level managers, we could learn much about the actual reasons for such an impact by interviewing a well-selected number of managers across firms. The numbers of those interviews will not be too large, interviews will most likely be semi-structured (the researchers will have an initial set of questions, but the communication will be two-way and relatively free-flowing), and the researcher will look for key, qualitative, concepts and ideas. Interviews can also prove especially powerful when the empirical puzzle in question is rather "micro" in nature and difficult to quantify.

As a third example, consider the coding or simple examination of texts, documents, and transcripts of meetings and events. A number of excellent recent studies of policy shifts and decision-making at organizations such as the World Bank, the IMF, the WTO, and the United States Federal Reserve Bank rely on such tools. What are the advantages and limitations of these tools? When are they likely to be deployed with success? Recall, for instance, Abolafia's (2005) examination of how key decision-makers at the Federal Reserve Bank of the United States interpret economic data and problems, and generate possible solutions. Abolafia discussed the importance of existing conceptual frameworks, familiar narratives, and expectations about the public's reaction. The object of investigation is relatively contained or small, record-keeping (conversations are recorded and transcribed, decisions are recorded, etc.) is systematic and reliable, and key information is accessible. These sorts of investigations are likely to yield insights into organizations and other types of actors, and the sort of institutions that structure or emerge out of them.

Much more needs to be said, then, about each methodological approach. Now, such an overview would be challenging to produce in the case of a well-established discipline with clear boundaries. The classic work of scholars such as Theda Skocpol (1984) in the realm of comparative historical sociology, for instance, has been so impressive precisely because of the magnitude of the task being tackled. In the case of economic sociology and institutional analyses, such clear boundaries still do not exist. In this book, we deliberately limited our discussion to the impact of institutions on the economic behavior of individuals and organizations, the economies of nation-states, and the international economy. We made the economy, in other words, the dependent variable of interest. But many economic sociologists, as we already noted, actually operate in a different fashion. Some are interested in how change occurs in societal institutions linked to the global economy. Others are eager to understand how the economy (a fiscal crisis, for example) affects societal institutions (labor-market policies, for example). Yet others wish to know more about the origins and demise of institutions. All this complicates matters. Any exploration of methodologies would need to take into account such undefined disciplinary boundaries and begin, perhaps, by asking whether particular methodologies may be best for particular fields of inquiry.

E. Institutions and Change

A considerable amount of effort over the last 30 years has gone into explaining institutional change – with economic sociologists, but also, and perhaps more dominantly until recently, political scientists contributing to the debate. As Campbell recently pointed out, the early works focused on technological or functional imperatives driving change, while the more recent works have paid more attention to actors (Campbell 2010b). The latter approach developed partly in tandem with the recognition that institutions are always contested, and that various stakeholders, endowed with differential amounts of power, are inevitably attempting to change those institutions in their favor. The literature is at this point quite well developed. Institutions may evolve in a path-dependent fashion. They may change in order to complement each other. And they may be connected with each other in such a way that a change in one will affect a change in another (Morgan et al. 2010). Actors are involved in all of these processes. Yet, as Campbell himself recently noted, most of the existing research has focused on national-level economies (Campbell 2010b: 109).

Institutional dynamics at the international level must be brought squarely into the research agenda of economic sociology. This should happen with at least three different sorts of issues in mind. First, institutions operating at the international level affect the international economy. If we wish to understand changes in the latter, we must account for changes in the former. And we must also account for how, exactly, changes in the former translate into changes in the latter: through what mechanisms? Are there mediating variables (such as other institutions, but also technology, interests, culture, and so on) that affect that impact? One obvious place to start would be RTAs. The EU but also blocs such as Mercosur, ASEAN's Free Trade Area, Caricom, COMESA, and others have undergone major changes in their foundational agreements and frameworks, with often far-reaching consequences for regional trade, the expansion of transnational companies, labor movement, and much more. We know too little, in comparative terms, about what brings about those changes and what shapes their impact on the international economy. At a more abstract level, dominant paradigms (such as the neoliberal Washington Consensus of the 1980s and later decades) influence – through their articulation via bodies such as the IMF or the World Bank – to a great extent how much and how rapidly capital and goods move across national borders. What accounts for changes in those paradigms? And what factors (for instance, politics) mediate the impact of those changes on actual international economic activity? There is then a large number of multilateral trade agreements, declarations, and frameworks that also deserves close examination.

Second, institutions at the international level affect national economies. The WTO, IMF, and the World Bank offer obvious examples. Changes in the policies and programs of those organizations have major implications for national economies. What, then, drives such change? And, crucially, how does such change translate into domestic, national-level change? Consider, for instance, the Basel II Framework, an agreement among leaders from 27 of the most important economies in the world concerning capital requirements for banks. Originally published in 2004, it underwent several revisions (until it was superseded by Basel III in late 2010 in response to the financial crisis of 2008–9). Basel II had implications not only for banks operating in a given country, but, as a result of this, for the availability of credit, and the extent and distribution of risk in domestic economies. All of these, in turn, affected the operations of everything from small to very large enterprises. What sorts of factors – institutional but also cultural, political, economic, and even technological – explain the revisions introduced to Basel II over the years? And how did national-level factors affect the exact implementation (extent, quality, etc.) of the accord in each country? Transnational rule-making (formal and informal) is perhaps the most important institutional variable that we wish to scrutinize for change and its impact on national economies.

Many other international institutions of relevance for national economies deserve closer scrutiny, of course. These include international statistical and ranking benchmarks (such as those of the Organization for Economic Cooperation and Development), the functioning of international tribunals (especially for trade dispute resolutions), and dominant paradigms in world society about the structure and policies of modern and successful corporations.

Third, national-level institutions are often closely connected to international-level institutions. Consider the EU as a case in point. National legal systems in the EU context have been highly affected by the arrival of EU law. Soft law at the international level has affected national law, but also institutions such as industry-level standards, informal but deeply entrenched standard operating procedures in firms as well as public-sector agencies, the programs and policies of lobbying groups, and much more. The EU's funding policies for relatively poor areas in the member-states, in turn, have strengthened subnational regional administrative structures and regional development programs. All these connections between institutions have impacted national economic life.

Or consider "blueprints" – that is, sets of instructions – in world society about the attributes of modern, Western nation-states. Those blueprints make it nearly imperative for the education system of those countries to be secular and universal, offering instruction in scientific, humanistic, and artistic disciplines (Kamens and Meyer 1996). This has shaped in profound ways the skills and knowledge found in the labor pool, how education is funded, and who the providers of education must be. But these blueprints shift, and this causes shifts in national-level institutions, and – via a number of mechanisms – changes in economic life. To date, we lack systematic frameworks for grasping in partial or comprehensive ways the connections between national and international institutions, their impact on economic life, and how change figures in all of these relationships. No single framework can, of course, provide all the answers. Much could be gained, however, from developing even tentative and competing frameworks.

Concluding Remarks

Economic sociology is a relatively young discipline. Institutionalist approaches within that discipline are younger still. A significant body of groundbreaking research is nonetheless developing. This book is an attempt to make sense of – clarify, order, and at times evaluate – that body of research. It was certainly limited in scope: it dealt only with the "informal and formal rules and practices" that affect economic life. And it concerned itself mostly with the role of institutions in shaping and enabling economic life. Some sociologists embrace different definitions of institutions, and assign to them rather different roles. They are also interested in more than how institutions affect the economy, as just noted a few pages ago. Future analyses can certainly focus on those works: their scope, contributions, and limitations. The objective of this book was thus quite simple: to shed light on some of the most central and exciting concepts in the emerging institutionalist research in economic sociology.

References

Abdelal, Rawi. 2007. *Global Rules: The Construction of Global Finance*. Ithaca, NY: Cornell University Press.

Abolafia, Mitchel Y. 2001. *Making Markets: Opportunism and Restraint on Wall Street*. Cambridge, MA: Harvard University Press.

Abolafia, Mitchel Y. 2005. "Making Sense of Recession: Toward an Interpretative Theory of Economic Action." In *The Economic Sociology of Capitalism*. Nee, Victor, and Richard Swedberg, eds. Princeton, NJ: Princeton University Press, pp. 204–26.

Adams, Samuel, and Berhanu Mengistu. 2008. "The Political Economy of Privatization in Sub-Saharan Africa." *Social Science Quarterly* 89: 78–94.

Aguilera, Ruth V. 2005. "Corporate Governance and Director Accountability: An Institutional Comparative Perspective." *British Journal of Management* 16: 39–53.

Aguilera, Ruth V., and Gregory Jackson. 2003. "The Cross-National Diversity of Corporate Governance: Dimensions and Determinants." *Academy of Management Review* 28: 447–65.

Aguilera, Ruth V., and Gregory Jackson. 2010. "Comparative and International Corporate Governance." *Annals of the Academy of Management* 4: 485–556.

Aldcroft, Derek H. 2007. "The Fatal Inversion: The African Growth Disaster." In *Economic Disasters of the Twentieth Century*. Oliver, Michael J., and Derek H. Aldcroft, eds. Northampton, MA: Edward Elgar, pp. 312–48.

Almeling, Rene. 2007. "Selling Genes, Selling Gender: Egg Agencies, Sperm Banks, and the Medical Market in Genetic Material." *American Sociological Review* 72: 319–40.

Amable, Bruno. 2000. "Institutional Complementarity and Diversity of Social Systems of Innovation and Production." *Review of International Political Economy* 7: 645–87.

Anderson, Terry L., and Fred S. McChesney, eds. 2003. *Private Property: Cooperation, Conflict, and Law*. Princeton, NJ: Princeton University Press.

References

Argote, Linda, et al. 2000. "Knowledge Transfer in Organizations: Learning from the Experience of Others." *Organizational Behavior and Human Decision Processes* 82: 1–8.

Aristotle. 1999. *Metaphysics.* Oxford and New York: Oxford University Press.

Armour, John, and Simon Deakin. 2003. "Insolvency and Employment Protection: The Mixed Effects of the Acquired Rights Directive." *International Review of Law and Economics* 22: 443–63.

Armour, John, et al. 2003. "Shareholder Primacy and the Trajectory of UK Corporate Governance." *British Journal of Industrial Relations* 41: 531–55.

Arrow, Kenneth J. 1974. *The Limits of Organization.* New York: Norton.

Ashforth, Blake E., and Barrie W. Gibbs. 1990. "The Double-Edge of Organizational Legitimation." *Organization Science* 1: 177–94.

Backhouse, Roger E., and Steven G. Medema. 2009. "Retrospectives: On the Definition of Economics." *Journal of Economic Perspectives* 23: 221–33.

Bacon, Christopher M., et al. 2008. "Are Sustainable Coffee Certifications Enough to Secure Farmer Livelihoods? The Millenium Development Goals and Nicaragua's Fair Trade Cooperatives." *Globalizations* 5: 259–74.

Baer, Hans A. 2006. "The Drive for Legitimation in Australian Naturopathy: Successes and Dilemmas." *Social Science & Medicine* 63: 1771–83.

Bandelj, Nina. 2008. *From Communists to Foreign Capitalists: The Social Foundations of Foreign Direct Investment in Postsocialist Europe.* Princeton, NJ: Princeton University Press.

Banerjee, Abhijit, and Lakshmi Iyer. 2005. "History, Institutions, and Economic Performance: The Legacy of Colonial Land Tenure Systems in India." *American Economic Review* 95: 1190–213.

Bartley, Tim. 2003. "Certifying Forests and Factories: States, Social Movements, and the Rise of Private Regulation in the Apparel and Forest Products Fields." *Politics & Society* 31: 433.

Bartunek, Jean, et al. 2003. "Sharing and Expanding Academic and Practitioner Knowledge in Health Care." *Journal of Health Services Research and Policy* 8: 62–8.

Bate, Paul. 2000. "Changing the Culture of a Hospital: From Hierarchy to Networked Community." *Public Administration* 78: 485–512.

Bendor, Jonathan, et al. 2001. "Recycling the Garbage Can: An Assessment of the Research Program." *American Political Science Review* 95: 169–90.

Benjamin, Beth A., and Joel M. Podolny. 1999. "Status, Quality, and Social Order in the California Wine Industry." *Administrative Science Quarterly* 44: 563–89.

Berg, Ivar, and Arne L. Kalleberg, eds. 2001. *Sourcebook of Labor Markets: Evolving Structures and Processes.* New York: Kluwer Academic/Plenum Publishers.

Best, Jacqueline. 2010. "Bringing Power Back in: The IMF's New Constructivist Strategy in Critical Perspective." In *Constructing the International Economy.* Blyth, Mark, et al., eds. Ithaca, NY: Cornell University Press, pp. 107–27.

References

Bialous, Stella A., and Derek Yach. 2001. "Whose Standard Is It, Anyway? How the Tobacco Industry Determines the International Organization for Standardization (ISO) Standards for Tobacco and Tobacco Products." *Tobacco Control* 10: 96–104.

Biggart, Nicole Woolsey, and Mauro F. Guillén. 1999. "Developing Difference: Social Organization and the Rise of the Auto Industries of South Korea, Taiwan, Spain, and Argentina." *American Sociological Review* 64: 722–47.

Blau, Judith R., et al. 1985. "Social Inequality and the Arts." *American Journal of Sociology* 91: 309–31.

Block, Fred, and Matthew R. Keller. 2009. "Where Do Innovations Come From? Transformations in the US Economy, 1970–2006." *Socio-Economic Review* 7: 459–83.

Boland, Richard J., Jr., and Ramkrishnan V. Tenkasi. 1995. "Perspective Making and Perspective Taking in Communities of Knowing." *Organization Science* 6: 350–72.

Boli, John, and George M. Thomas. 1997. "World Culture in the World Polity: A Century of International Non-Governmental Organization." *American Sociological Review* 62: 171–90.

Boli, John, and George M. Thomas. 1999. "NGOs and the Organization of World Culture." In *Constructing World Culture: International Nongovernmental Organizations Since 1875*. Boli, John, and George M. Thomas, eds. California: Stanford University Press, pp. 13–49.

Borrás, Susana, and Dimitrios Tsagdis. 2008. *Cluster Policies in Europe: Firms, Institutions and Governance*. Cheltenham, UK: Edward Elgar Publishing.

Börzel, Tanja A., and Thomas Risse. 2003. "Conceptualising the Domestic Impact of Europe." In *The Politics of Europeanization*. Featherstone, Kevin, and Claudio M. Radelli, eds. Oxford: Oxford University Press, pp. 57–81.

Botzem, Sebastian, and Sigrid Quack. 2006. "Contested Rules and Shifting Boundaries: International Standard-Setting in Accounting." In *Transnational Governance: Institutional Dynamics of Regulation*. Djelic, Marie-Laure, and Kerstin Sahlin-Andersson, eds. New York: Cambridge University Press, pp. 266–86.

Bourdieu, Pierre. 1984. *Distinction: A Social Critique of the Judgement of Taste*. Cambridge, MA: Harvard University Press.

Brett, E. A. 2008. "State Failure and Success in Uganda and Zimbabwe: The Logic of Political Decay and Reconstruction in Africa." *Journal of Development Studies* 44: 339–64.

Bridges, William P., and Robert L. Nelson. 2001. "Economic and Sociological Approaches to Gender Inequality in Pay." In *The Sociology of Economic Life*. Granovetter, Mark, and Richard Swedberg, eds. Boulder, CO: Westview, pp. 163–90.

Brinton, Mary C., and Victor Nee, eds. 1998. *The New Institutionalism in Sociology*. New York: Russell Sage Foundation.

References

Brown, Andrew D. 1998. "Narrative, Politics and Legitimacy in an IT Implementation." *Journal of Management Studies* 35: 35–58.

Brown, John Seely, and Paul Duguid. 1991. "Organizational Learning and Communities-of-Practice: Toward a Unified View of Working, Learning, and Innovation." *Organization Science* 2: 40–57.

Brunsson, Nils, and Bengt Jacobsson. 2000. "The Contemporary Expansion of Standardization." In *A World of Standards*. Brunsson, Nils, and Bengt Jacobsson, eds. New York: Oxford University Press, pp. 1–17.

Brunssons, Nils, and Bengt Jacobsson, eds. 2000. *A World of Standards*. New York: Oxford University Press.

Burr, Thomas. 2006. "Building Community, Legitimating Consumption: Creating the U.S. Bicycle Market, 1876–1884." *Socio-Economic Review* 4: 417–46.

Burroni, Luigi, et al. 2008. "Local Economic Governance in Hard Times: The Shadow Economy and the Textile and Clothing Industries Around Łódź and Naples." *Socio-Economic Review* 6: 473–92.

Butler, Jr., John K. 1999. "Trust Expectations, Information Sharing, Climate of Trust, and Negotiation Effectiveness." *Group & Organization Management* 24: 217–38.

Cameron, David. 1998. "Creating Supranational Authority in Monetary and Exchange Rate Policy: The Sources and Effects of EMU." In *European Integration and Supranational Governance*. Sandholtz, Wayne, and Alec Stone Sweet, eds. Oxford: Oxford University Press, pp. 188–216.

Campbell, John L. 1989. "Corporations, Collective Organization, and the State: Industry Response to the Accident at Three Mile Island." *Social Science Quarterly* 70: 650–66.

Campbell, John L. 2003. "States, Politics and Globalization: Why Institutions Still Matter." In *The Nation-State in Question*. Paul, T.V., et al., eds. Princeton, NJ: Princeton University Press, pp. 234–59.

Campbell, John L. 2004. *Institutional Change and Globalization*. Princeton, NJ: Princeton University Press.

Campbell, John L. 2007. "Why Would Corporations Behave in Socially Responsible Ways? An Institutional Theory of Corporate Social Responsibility." *Academy of Management Review* 32: 946–67.

Campbell, John L. 2010a. "Neoliberalism in Crisis: Regulatory Roots of the U.S. Financial Meltdown." *Research in the Sociology of Organizations* 30B: 65–101.

Campbell, John L. 2010b. "Institutional Reproduction and Change." In *Oxford Handbook of Comparative Institutional Analysis*. Morgan, Glenn, et al., eds. New York: Oxford University Press, pp. 87–115.

Campbell, John L, and Leon N. Lindberg 1990. "Property Rights and the Organization of Economic Activity by the State." *American Sociological Review* 5: 634–47.

References

Campbell, John L., and Ove K. Pedersen. 2007. "The Varieties of Capitalism and Hybrid Success: Denmark in the Global Economy." *Comparative Political Studies* 40: 307–32.

Campbell, John L., and John A. Hall. 2009. "National Identity and the Political Economy of Small States." *Review of International Political Economy* 16: 547–72.

Caporaso, James, et al., eds. 2001. *Transforming Europe: Europeanization and Domestic Change*. Ithaca, NY: Cornell University Press.

Carolan, Michael S. 2008. "From Patent Law to Regulation: The Ontological Gerrymandering of Biotechnology." *Environmental Politics* 17: 749–65.

Carruthers, Bruce G., and Laura Ariovich. 2004. "The Sociology of Property Rights." *Annual Review of Sociology* 30: 23–46.

Carruthers, Bruce G., and Sarah L. Babb. 1999. *Economy/Society: Markets, Meaning and Social Structure*. Thousand Oaks, CA: Pine Forge Press.

Centeno, Miguel Angel. 1994. "Between Rocky Democracies and Hard Markets: Dilemmas of the Double Transition." *Annual Review of Sociology* 20: 125–47.

Centeno, Miguel A., and Joseph N, Cohen. 2010. *Global Capitalism*. Cambridge: Polity.

Cetina, Karin Knorr, and Alex Preda, eds. 2004. *The Sociology of Financial Markets*. Oxford: Oxford University Press.

Chase-Dunn, Christopher. 1989. *Global Formations: Structures of the World-Economy*. Cambridge: Blackwell.

Chibber, Vivek. 2002. "Bureaucratic Rationality and the Developmental State." *American Journal of Sociology* 107: 951–89.

Chorev, Nitsan, and Sarah Babb. 2009. "The Crisis of Neoliberalism and the Future of International Institutions: A Comparison of the IMF and the WTO." *Theory and Society* 38: 459–84.

Coatsworth, John H. 2008. "Inequality, Institutions and Economic Growth in Latin America." *Journal of Latin American Studies* 40: 545–69.

Cohen, Michael D., et al. 1972. "A Garbage Can Model of Organizational Choice." *Administrative Science Quarterly* 17: 1–25.

Cohen, Michael D., et al. 1979. "People, Problems, Solutions and the Ambiguity of Relevance." In *Ambiguity and Choice in Organizations*. March, James G., and Johan P. Olsen, eds. Norway: Scandinavian University Press, pp. 24–37.

Commons, John R. 1931. "Institutional Economics." *American Economic Review* 21: 648– 57.

Cook, Karen, S., ed. 2001. *Trust in Society*. New York: Russell Sage Foundation.

Corbett, Charles J., and David A. Kirsch. 2001. "International Diffusion of ISO 14000 Certification." *Production and Operations Management* 10: 327–42.

Crouch, Colin. 2005. *Capitalist Diversity and Change: Recombinant Governance and Institutional Entrepreneurs*. Oxford: Oxford University Press.

Culpepper, Pepper D. 2010. *Quiet Politics and Business Power: Corporate Control in Europe and Japan*. Cambridge: Cambridge University Press.

References

Currie, Graeme, and Olga Suhomlinova. 2006. "The Impact of Institutional Forces Upon Knowledge Sharing in the UK NHS: The Triumph of Professional Power and the Inconsistency of Policy." *Public Administration* 84: 1–30.

Dagdeviren, Hulya, et al. 2002. "Poverty Reduction with Growth and Redistribution." *Development & Change* 33: 383–413.

Davis, Gerald F., and Christopher Marquis. 2005. "The Globalization of Stock Markets and Convergence in Corporate Governance." In *The Economic Sociology of Capitalism*. Nee, Victor, and Richard Swedberg, eds. Princeton, NJ: Princeton University Press, pp. 352–90.

Deakin, Simon. 2009. "Legal Origin, Juridical Form and Industrialization in Historical Perspective: The Case of the Employment Contract and the Joint-Stock Company." *Socio-Economic Review* 7: 35–65.

Deakin, Simon, and Prabirjit Sarkar. 2008. "Assessing the Long-Run Economic Impact of Labour Law Systems: A Theoretical Reappraisal and Analysis of New Time Series Data." *Industrial Relations Journal* 39: 453–87.

Deephouse, David L. 1996. "Does Isomorphism Legitimate." *Academy of Management Journal* 39: 1024–39.

De Long, David W., and Liam Fahey. 2000. "Diagnosing Cultural Barriers to Knowledge Management." *Academy of Management Executive* 14: 113–27.

DiMaggio, Paul, ed. 2001. *The Twenty-First-Century Firm: Changing Economic Organization in International Perspective*. Princeton, NJ: Princeton University Press.

DiMaggio, Paul J., and Walter W. Powell. 1983. "The Iron Cage Revisited: Institutional Isomorphism and Collective Rationality in Organizational Fields." *American Sociological Review* 47: 147–60.

Djelic, Marie-Laure. 1998. *Exporting the American Model. The Postwar Transformation of European Business*. Oxford: Oxford University Press.

Djelic, Marie-Laure, and Kerstin Sahlin-Andresson, eds. 2008. *Transnational Governance: Institutional Dynamics of Regulation*. Cambridge: Cambridge University Press.

Dobbin, Frank, ed. 2004a. *The New Economic Sociology: A Reader*. Princeton, NJ: Princeton University Press.

Dobbin, Frank. 2004b. "Introduction: The Sociology of the Economy." In *The New Economic Sociology: A Reader*. Dobbin, Frank, ed. Princeton, NJ: Princeton University Press, pp. 1–25.

Dobbin, Frank, and Timothy J. Dowd. 2000. "The Market that Antitrust Built: Public Policy, Private Coercion, and Railroad Acquisitions, 1825 to 1922." *American Sociological Review* 65: 631–57.

Dobbin, Frank, and John R. Sutton. 1998. "The Strength of a Weak State: The Rights Revolution and the Rise of Human Resources Management Divisions." *American Journal of Sociology* 104: 441–76.

References

Downs, Anthony. 1957. *An Economic Theory of Democracy.* New York: Harper.
Duffield, John. 2007. "What Are International Institutions?" *International Studies Review* 9: 1–22.
Duina, Francesco. 1999. *Harmonizing Europe: Nation States within the Common Market.* Albany, NY: SUNY Press.
Duina, Francesco. 2006. *The Social Construction of Free Trade: The European Union, NAFTA, and Mercosur.* Princeton, NJ: Princeton University Press.
Duina, Francesco. 2010. "Frames, Scripts, and the Making of Regional Trade Agreements." In *Constructing the International Economy.* Blyth, Mark, et al., eds. Ithaca, NY: Cornell University Press, pp. 107–27.
Duina, Francesco, and Jason Buxbaum. 2008. "Regional Trade Agreements and the Pursuit of State Interests: Institutional Perspectives from NAFTA and Mercosur." *Economy and Society* 37: 193–223.
Duina, Francesco, and Michael Oliver. 2005. "National Parliaments in the European Union: Are There Any Benefits to Integration?" *European Law Journal* 11: 173–95.
Edelman, Lauren B. 1990. "Legal Environments and Organizational Governance: The Expansion of Due Process in the American Workplace." *American Journal of Sociology* 95: 1401–40.
Edigheji, O'mano Emma. 1999. "The Institutional Mediation of Globalization: Reconceptualizing the Role of the State in the Post-Development Era." *Society in Transition* 30: 106–19.
Epping, Randing Charles. 2001. *A Beginner's Guide to the World Economy.* New York: Vintage Books.
Espeland, Wendy Nelson, and Michael Sauder. 2007. "Rankings and Reactivity: How Public Measures Recreate Social Worlds." *American Journal of Sociology* 113: 1–40.
Evans, Peter. 1995. *Embedded Autonomy: States and Industrial Transformation.* Princeton, NJ: Princeton University Press.
Falkner, Gerda, et al. 2004. "Non-Compliance with EU Directives in the Member States: Opposition through the Backdoor?" *West European Politics* 27: 452–73.
Falkner, Gerda, et al. 2005. *Complying with Europe: EU Harmonisation and Soft Law in the Member States.* New York: Cambridge University Press.
Fashoyin, Tayo. 2004. "Tripartite Cooperation, Social Dialogue and National Development." *International Labour Review* 143: 341–71.
Feld, Werner J., et al. 1983. *International Organizations: A Comparative Approach.* New York: Praeger Publishers.
Fernandez, Roberto M., et al. 2000. "Social Capital at Work: Networks and Employment at a Phone Center." *American Journal of Sociology* 105: 1288–356.
Finnemore, Martha. 1996. "Norms, Culture, and World Politics: Insights from Sociology's Institutionalism." *International Organization* 50: 325–47.

References

Fligstein, Neil. 1990. *The Transformation of Corporate Control*. Cambridge, MA: Harvard University Press.

Fligstein, Neil. 1991. "The Structural Transformation of American Industry: An Institutional Account of the Causes of Diversification in the Largest Firms, 1919–1979." In *The New Institutionalism in Organizational Analysis*. Powell, Walter W., and Paul J. DiMaggio, eds. Chicago, IL: University of Chicago Press, pp. 311–36.

Fligstein, Neil. 1996. "Markets as Politics: A Political–cultural Approach to Market Institutions." *American Sociological Review* 61: 656–73.

Fligstein, Neil. 2001. *The Architecture of Markets: An Economic Sociology of Twenty-First-Century Capitalist Societies*. Princeton, NJ: Princeton University Press.

Fligstein, Neil. 2004. "From the Transformation of Corporate Control." In *The New Economic Sociology: A Reader*. Dobbin, Frank, ed. Princeton, NJ: Princeton University Press, pp. 407–32.

Fligstein, Neil, and Iona Mara-Drita. 1996. "How to Make a Market: Reflections on the Attempt to Create a Single Market in the European Union." *American Journal of Sociology* 102: 1–33.

Fligstein, Neil, and Jason McNichol. 1998. "The Institutional Terrain of the European Union." In *European Integration and Supranational Governance*. Sandholtz, Wayne, and Alec Stone Sweet, eds. New York: Oxford University Press, pp. 59–91.

Fourcade-Gourinchas, Marion, and Sarah L. Babb. 2002. "The Rebirth of the Liberal Creed: Paths to Neoliberalism in Four Countries." *American Journal of Sociology* 108: 533–79.

Frank, Andre Gunder. 1969. *Capitalism and Underdevelopment in Latin America: Historical Studies of Chile and Brazil*. New York: Monthly Review Press.

Frank, David John, et al. 2000. "The Nation-State and the Natural Environment over the Twentieth Century." *American Sociological Review* 65: 96–116.

Friedman, Milton. 1962. *Capitalism and Freedom*. Chicago, IL: University of Chicago Press.

Friedman, Milton. 1980. *Free to Choose: A Personal Statement*. New York: Harcourt Brace Jovanovich.

Furubotn, Eirik G., and Rudolf Richter. 2005. *Institutions and Economic Theory: The Contribution of the New Institutional Economics*. Ann Arbor, MI: University of Michigan Press.

Furusten, Staffan. 2000. "The Knowledge Base of Standards." In *A World of Standards*. Brunsson, Nils, and Bengt Jacobsson, eds. New York: Oxford University Press, pp. 71–99.

Galaskiewicz, Joseph. 1985. "Professional Networks and the Institutionalization of a Single Mind Set." *American Sociological Review* 50: 639–58.

References

Galaskiewicz, Jospeh. 1991. "Making Corporate Actors Accountable; Institution-Building in Minneapolis-St. Paul." In *The New Institutionalism in Organizational Analysis*. Powell, Walter W., and Paul J. DiMaggio, eds. Chicago, IL: The University of Chicago Press, pp. 293–312.

Gallhofer, Sonjand, and Jim Haslam. 2007. "Exploring Social, Political and Economic Dimensions of Accounting in the Global Context: The International Accounting Standards Board and Accounting Disaggregation." *Socio-Economic Review* 5: 633–64.

Garcia-Parpet, Marie-France. 2008. "Markets, Prices and Symbolic Value: Grands Crus and the Challenges of Global Markets." *International Review of Sociology* 18: 237–52.

Geertz, Clifford. 1973. *The Interpretation of Cultures*. New York: Basic Books.

Geertz, Clifford. 2001. "The Bazaar Economy: Information and Search in Peasant Marketing." In *The Sociology of Economic Life*. Granovetter, Mark, and Richard Swedberg, eds. Boulder, CO: Westview Press, pp. 139–45.

Gereffi, Gary, and Stephanie Fonda. 1992. "Regional Paths of Development." *Annual Review of Sociology* 18: 419–48.

Ginsburg, Tom. 2000. "Does Law Matter for Economic Development? Evidence From East Asia." *Law & Society Review* 34: 829–56.

Gjølberg, Maria. 2009. "The Origin of Corporate Social Responsibility: Global Forces or National Legacies?" *Socio-Economic Review* 7: 605–37.

Glenn, John K. 2004. "From Nation-States to Member States: Accession Negotiations as an Instrument of Europeanization." *Comparative European Politics* 2: 3–28.

Goyer, Michel. 2011. *Contingent Capital: Short-term Investors and the Evolution of Corporate Governance in France and Germany*. Oxford: Oxford University Press.

Granovetter, Mark. 1985. "Economic Action and Social Structure: The Problem of Embeddedness." *American Journal of Sociology* 91: 481–510.

Granovetter, Mark, and Richard Swedberg, eds. 2001. *The Sociology of Economic Life*. Boulder, CO: Westview Press.

Greenfeld, Liah. 2006. *Nationalism and the Mind: Essays on Modern Culture*. Oxford: Oneworld Publications.

Gregory, Sean. 2009. "Are Direct-to-Consumer Drug Ads Doomed?" *Time Magazine*, February 4.

Greuning, Hennie van. 2009. *International Financial Reporting Standards: A Practical Guide*. Washington, DC: The World Bank.

Guillen, Mauro F., et al., eds. 2002. *The New Economic Sociology: Developments in an Emerging Field*. New York: Sage Publications.

Hacker, Jacob S., and Paul Pierson. 2007. "Tax Politics and the Struggle Over Activist Government." In *The Transformation of American Politics: Activist Government and the Rise of Conservatism*. Pierson, Paul, and Theda Skocpol, eds. Princeton, NJ: Princeton University Press, pp. 256–80.

References

Haggard, Stephan. 1990. *Pathways from the Periphery: The Politics of Growth in the Newly Industrializing Countries.* Ithaca, NY: Cornell University Press.

Hall, Hazel. 2001. "Input-Friendliness: Motivating Knowledge Sharing Across Intranets." *Journal of Information Science* 27: 139–46.

Hall, Peter A. 1986. *Governing the Economy: The Politics of State Intervention in Britain and France.* New York: Oxford University Press.

Hall, Peter A., and David Soskice. 2001. "Introduction." In *Varieties of Capitalism: The Institutional Foundations of Comparative Advantage.* Hall, Peter A., and David Soskice, eds. New York: Oxford University Press, pp. 1–68.

Hall, Peter A., and Kathleen Thelen. 2009. "Institutional Change in Varieties of Capitalism." *Socio-Economic Review* 7: 7–34.

Hamilton, Elizabeth A. 2006. "An Exploration of the Relationship between Loss of Legitimacy and the Sudden Death of Organizations." *Group and Organization Management* 3: 327–58.

Hamilton, Gary G., and Biggart, Nicole Woosley. 2001. "Market, Culture, and Authority: A Comparative Analysis of Management and Organization in the Far East." In *The Sociology of Economic Life.* Granovetter, Mark, and Richard Swedberg, eds. Boulder, CO: Westview Press, pp. 444–77.

Hatanaka, Maki, and Lawrence Busch. 2008. "Third-Party Certification in the Global Agrifood System: An Objective or Socially Mediated Governance Mechanism?" *Sociologia Ruralis* 48: 73–91.

Haverland, Markus. 2000. "National Adaptation to European Integration: The Importance of Institutional Veto Points." *Journal of Public Policy* 20: 83–103.

Healy, Kieran. 1999. "The Emergence of HIV in the U.S. Blood Supply: Organizations, Obligations and the Management of Uncertainty." *Theory and Society* 28: 529–58.

Helfer, Laurence R., et al. 2008. "Islands of Effective International Adjudication: Constructing an Intellectual Property Rule of Law in CAN." Unpublished manuscript.

Henley, Andrew, and Euclid Tsakalotos. 1992. "Corporatism and the European Labour Market after 1992." *British Journal of Industrial Relations* 30: 567–86.

Herrmann, Andrea R. 2008. "Rethinking the Link Between Labour Market Flexibility and Corporate Competitiveness: A Critique of the Institutionalist Literature." *Socio-Economic Review* 6: 637–69.

Hicks, Alexander, and Lane Kenworthy. 1998. "Cooperation and Political Economic Performance in Affluent Democratic Capitalism." *American Journal of Sociology* 103: 1631–72.

Hirschman, Albert O. 1977. *The Passions and the Interests: Political Arguments for Capitalism before Its Triumph.* Princeton, NJ: Princeton University Press.

References

Hirst, Paul, and Grahame Thompson. 2009. *Globalization in Question.* Cambridge: Polity.

Hollingsworth, J. Rogers, and Robert Boyer, eds. 1998. *Contemporary Capitalism: The Embeddedness of Institutions.* Cambridge: Cambridge University Press.

Howley, Kerry. 2006. "Absolution in Your Cup." *Reason* 37: 40–8.

Huber, Evelyne, and John D. Stephens. 2005. "State Economic and Social Policy in Global Capitalism." In *A Handbook of Political Sociology: States, Civil Societies, and Globalization.* Janoski, Thomas, et al., eds. New York: Cambridge University Press, pp. 607–29.

Huerta, Luis A. 2009. "Institutional v. Technical Environments: Reconciling the Goals of Decentralization in an Evolving Charter School Organization." *Peabody Journal of Education* 83: 244–61.

Hunt, Alan. 1996. "The Governance of Consumption: Sumptuary Laws and Shifting Forms of Regulation." *Economy & Society* 25: 410–27.

Inglehart, Ronald, and Wayne E. Baker. 2000. "Modernization, Cultural Change, and the Persistence of Traditional Values." *American Sociological Review* 65: 19–51.

Inkeles, Alex, and David Horton Smith. 1974. *Becoming Modern: Individual Change in Six Developing Countries.* Cambridge, MA: Harvard University Press.

ISO. 2010. "TC 126." *International Organization for Standardization.* Available at: <http://www.iso.org/iso/standards_development/technical_committees/list_of_iso_technical_committees/iso_technical_committee.htm?commid=52158>.

Jacobsson, Bengt. 2006. "Regulated Regulators: Global Trends of State Transformation." In *Transnational Governance: Institutional Dynamics of Regulation.* Djelic, Marie-Laure, and Kerstin Sahlin-Andersson, eds. New York: Cambridge University Press, pp. 205–24.

Jacobsson, Bengt, and Kerstin Sahlin-Andersson. 2006. "Dynamics of Soft Regulations." In *Transnational Governance: Institutional Dynamics of Regulation.* Djelic, Marie-Laure, and Kerstin Sahlin-Andersson, eds. New York: Cambridge University Press, pp. 247–65.

Jensen, Nathan M. 2003. "Democratic Governance and Multinational Corporations: Political Regimes and Inflows of Foreign Direct Investment." *International Organization* 57: 587–616.

Jepperson, Ronald L., and John W. Meyer. 1991. "The Public Order and the Construction of Formal Organizations." In *The New Institutionalism in Organizational Analysis.* Powell, Walter W., and Paul J. DiMaggio, eds. Chicago, IL: The University of Chicago Press, pp. 204–31.

Kalev, Alexandra, et al. 2006. "Best Practices or Best Guesses? Assessing the Efficacy of Corporate Affirmative Action and Diversity Policies." *American Sociological Review* 71: 589–617.

Kamens, David H. 1977. "Legitimating Myths and Educational Organization: The Relationship Between Organizational Ideology and Formal Structure." *American Sociological Review* 42: 208–19.

References

Kamens, David H., and John W. Meyer. 1996. "Worldwide Patterns in Academic Secondary Education Curricula." *Comparative Education Review* 40: 116–38.

Karns, Margaret P., and Karen A. Mingst. 2004. *International Organizations: The Politics and Processes of Global Governance*. Boulder, CO: Lynne Rienner Publishers.

Keister, Lisa. 2000. *Chinese Business Groups: The Structure and Impact of Interfirm Relations During Economic Development*. New York: Oxford University Press.

Keister, Lisa A. 2008. "Conservative Protestants and Wealth: How Religion Perpetuates Asset Poverty." *American Journal of Sociology* 113: 1237–71.

Kim, Tae Kuen, and Karen Zurlo. 2009. "How Does Economic Globalisation Affect the Welfare State? Focusing on the Mediating Effect of Welfare Regimes." *International Journal of Social Welfare* 18: 130–41.

King, Lawrence. 2002. "Postcommunist Divergence: A Comparative Analysis of the Transition to Capitalism in Poland and Russia." *Studies in Comparative International Development* 37: 3–34.

Kingstone, Peter. 2006. "After the Washington Consensus: The Limits to Democratization and Development in Latin America." *Latin American Research Review* 41: 153–64.

Kite, Cynthia. 2002. "The Globalized, Generous Welfare State: Possibility or Oxymoron?" *European Journal of Political Research* 41: 307–43.

Köhler, Horst. 2001. "Standards and Codes: A Tool for Growth and Financial Stability. International Monetary Fund, March 7, 2001". Available at: <www.imf.org/external/np/speeches/2001/030701.htm>.

Kraatz, Matthew S., and Edward J. Zajac. 1996. "Exploring the Limits of the New Institutionalism: The Causes and Consequences of Illegitimate Organizational Change." *American Sociological Review* 61: 812–36.

Kramer, Roderick M., and Tom R. Tyler. 1996. *Trust in Organizations: Frontiers of Theory and Research*. Thousand Oaks, CA: Sage Publications.

Kuczynski, Pedro-Pablo, and John Williamson, eds. 2003. *After the Consensus: Restarting Growth and Reform in Latin America*. Washington, DC: Institute for International Economics.

Kus, Basak. 2006. "Neoliberalism, Institutional Change and the Welfare State: The Case of Britain and France." *International Journal of Comparative Sociology* 47: 488–525.

Kuwabara, Ko. 2005. "Affecting Attachment in Electronic Markets: The Case of Ebay." In *The Economic Sociology of Capitalism*. Nee, Victor, and Richard Swedberg, eds. Princeton, NJ: Princeton University Press, pp. 268–80.

Lane, Christel. 1998. "Introduction: Theories and Issues in the Study of Trust." In *Trust Within and Between Organizations: Conceptual Issues and Empirical Applications*. Lane, Christel, and Reinhard Bachmann, eds. Oxford: Oxford University Press, pp. 1–30.

References

Lee, Ming-Huang. 2008. "Tourism and Sustainable Livelihoods: The Case of Taiwan." *Third World Quarterly* 29: 961–78.

Lefter, Viorel, and Aureliana Geta Roman. 2007. "IAS 41 Agriculture: Fair Value Accounting." *Theoretical and Applied Economics* 5: 15–22.

Leiter, Jeffrey. 2008. "Nonprofit Isomorphism: An Australia–United States Comparison." *Voluntas: International Journal of Voluntary & Nonprofit Organizations* 19: 67–91.

Lerner, David. 1964. *The Passing of Traditional Society: Modernizing the Middle East.* Glencoe, IL: Free Press.

Levi, Margaret. 1988. *Of Rule and Revenue.* Berkeley and Los Angeles, CA: University of California Press.

Lewis, Peter. 2008. "Growth without Prosperity in Africa." *Journal of Democracy* 19: 95–109.

Lin, Nan, et al., eds. 2001. *Social Capital: Theory and Research.* New York: Aldine de Gruyter.

Linton, April, et al. 2004. "A Taste of Trade Justice: Marketing Global Social Responsibility via Fair Trade Coffee." *Globalizations* 1: 223–46.

Loya, Thomas A., and John Boli. 1999. "Standardization in the World Polity: Technical Rationality over Power." In *Constructing World Culture: International Nongovernmental Organizations Since 1875.* Boli, John, and George M. Thomas, eds. California: Stanford University Press, pp. 169–97.

Macaulay, Stewart. 1963. "Non-Contractual Relations in Business: A Preliminary Study." *American Sociological Review* 28: 1–23.

McDonough, Shelley Anne. 2007. *Risky Business: An Examination of Firm Location Decisions and Their Implications for Inner Cities.* Cambridge, MA: Dissertation Submitted to the Department of Sociology at Harvard University.

McDonough, Shelley. 2010. "Can We Seal the Deal?: An Examination of Uncertainty in the Development Process." *Economic Development Quarterly* 24: 87–96.

Macharia, Kinuthia. 1997. *Social and Political Dynamics of the Informal Economy in African Cities: Nairobi and Harare.* Lanham, MD: University Press of America.

McNally, Christopher A. 2007. "China's Capitalist Transition: The Making of a New Variety of Capitalism." *Comparative Social Research* 24: 177–203.

Mahoney, James. 2000. "Path Dependence in Historical Sociology." *Theory and Society* 24: 507–48.

Mansfield, Edward, D., and Helen V. Milner, eds. 1997. *The Political Economy of Regionalism.* New York: Columbia University Press.

Marchionini, Gary. 2002. "Co-Evolution of User and Organizational Interfaces: A Longitudinal Case Study of WWW Dissemination of National Statistics." *Journal of the American Society for Information Science and Technology* 53: 1192–1209.

References

Martin, Graham P., et al. 2009. "Reconfiguring or Reproducing Intra–Professional Boundaries? Specialist Expertise, Generalist Knowledge and the "Modernization" of the Medical Workforce." *Social Science and Medicine* 68: 1191–98.

Martin, Lisa L. 1993. "Credibility, Costs, and Institutions: Cooperation on Economic Sanctions." *World Politics* 45: 406–32.

Mastenbroek, Ellen, and Michael Kaeding. 2006. "Europeanization Beyond the Goodness of Fit: Domestic Politics in the Forefront." *Comparative European Politics* 4: 331–54.

Mattli, Walter, and Tim Büthe. 2003. "Setting International Standards: Technological Rationality or Primacy of Power?" *World Politics* 56: 1–42.

Mayer, Karl Ulrich, and Urs Schoepflin. 1989. "The State and the Life Course." *Annual Review of Sociology* 15: 187–209.

Meier, Henk Erik. 2008. "Institutional Complementarities and Institutional Dynamics: Exploring Varieties in European Football Capitalism." *Socio-Economic Review* 6: 99–133.

Meyer, John W. 1984. "Organizations as Ideological Systems." In *Leadership and Organizational Culture: New Perspectives on Administrative Theory and Practice*. Sergiovanni, Thomas J., and John E. Corbally, eds. Chicago, IL: University of Illinois Press, pp. 186–205.

Meyer, John W., and Brian Rowan. 1977. "Institutional Organizations: Formal Structure as Myth and Ceremony." *American Journal of Sociology* 83: 340–63.

Mizruchi, Mark S., et al. 2006. "The Conditional Nature of Embeddedness: A Study of Borrowing by Large U.S. Firms, 1973–1994." *American Sociological Review* 71: 310–33.

Mooney, Linda A., et al. 1992. "Legal Drinking Age and Alcohol Consumption." *Deviant Behavior* 13: 59–71.

Moravcsik, Andrew. 1998. *The Choice for Europe: Social Purpose and State Power from Messina to Maastricht*. Ithaca, NY: Cornell University Press.

Morgan, Glenn, 2001. "The Development of Transnational Standards and Regulations and their Impacts on Firms." In *The Multinational Firm: Organizing across Institutional and National Divides*. Morgan, Glenn, et al., eds. New York: Oxford University Press, pp. 225–52.

Morgan, Glenn et al., eds. 2010. *The Oxford Handbook of Comparative Institutional Analysis*. Oxford: Oxford University Press.

Mosley, Layna. 2000. "Room to Move: International Financial Markets and National Welfare States." *International Organization* 54: 737–73.

Mosley, Layna. 2008. "Global Production and Domestic Institutions in the Developing World." *Comparative Political Studies* 41: 674–714.

Mosley, Layna, and David Andrew Singer. 2008. "Taking Stock Seriously: Equity-Market Performance, Government Policy, and Financial Globalization." *International Studies Quarterly* 52: 405–25.

References

Mosley, Layna, and Saike Uno. 2007. "Racing to the Bottom or Climbing to the Top? Economic Globalization and Collective Labor Rights." *Comparative Political Studies* 40: 923–48.

Nadal, Alejandro. 2002. "Corn in NAFTA: Eight Years After." Montreal: North America Commission for Environmental Cooperation. Available at: <http://www.cec.org/files/pdf/ECONOMY/Corn–NAFTA_en.pdf>.

Nee, Victor, and Yang Cao. 1999. "Path Dependent Societal Transformation: Stratification in Hybrid Mixed Economies." *Theory & Society* 28: 799–834.

Nicholl, Peter. 2006. "Organisational Structures Do Matter for Good Governance and Good Performance." *Comparative Economic Studies* 48: 214–28.

North, Douglass C. 1990. *Institutions, Institutional Change and Economic Performance*. Cambridge: Cambridge University Press.

North, Douglass, and Robert Paul Thomas. 1973. *The Rise of the Western World: A New Economic History*. Cambridge: Cambridge University Press.

Nugent, Paul D., and Mitchel Y. Abolafia. 2006. "The Creation of Trust through Interaction and Exchange." *Group & Organization Management* 31: 628–50.

Odell, John S., ed. 2006. *Negotiating Trade: Developing Countries in the WTO and NATFA*. New York: Cambridge University Press.

Olsen, Johan P. 2001. "Garbage Cans, New Institutionalism, and the Study of Politics." *American Political Science Review* 95: 191–98.

Patterson, Orlando. 1982. *Slavery and Social Death: A Comparative Study*. Cambridge, MA: Harvard University Press.

Paul, T. V., et al., eds. 2003. *The Nation State in Question*. Princeton, NJ: Princeton University Press.

Pedersen, Jesper Strandgaard, and Frank Dobbin. 2006. "In Search of Identity and Legitimation: Bridging Organizational Culture and Neoinstitutionalism." *American Behavioral Scientist* 49: 897–907.

Pedersen, Ove K. 2010. "Institutional Competitiveness: How Nations Came to Compete." In *The Oxford Handbook of Comparative Institutional Analysis*. Morgan, Glenn, et al., eds. Oxford: Oxford University Press, pp. 625–57.

Peters, B. Guy. 2005. *Institutional Theory in Political Science*. London: Continuum.

Pierson, Paul. 1996. "The Path to European Integration." *Comparative Political Studies* 29: 123–64.

Pierson, Paul. 2004. *Politics in Time: History, Institutions, and Social Analysis*. Princeton, NJ: Princeton University Press.

Pierson, Paul, and Stephan Leibfried. 1995. "Multitiered Institutions and the Making of Social Policy." In *European Social Policy: Between Fragmentation and Integration*. Pierson, Paul, and Stephen Leibfried, eds. Washington, DC: The Brookings Institution, pp. 1–40.

Polanyi, Karl. 1944. "The Economy as Instituted Process." In *The Sociology of Economic Life*. Granovetter, Mark, and Richard Swedberg, eds. Boulder, CO: Westview Press, pp. 31–50.

References

Portes, Alejandro, and Bryan R. Roberts. 2005. "The Free-Market City: Latin American Urbanization in the Years of the Neoliberal Experiment." *Studies in Comparative International Development* 40: 43–82.

Portes, Alejandro, and Julia Sensenbrenner. 1993. "Embeddedness and Immigration: Notes on the Social Determinants of Economic Action." *American Journal of Sociology* 98: 1320–50.

Powell, Walter W., and Paul J. DiMaggio. 1991. *The New Institutionalism in Organizational Analysis*. Chicago, IL: University of Chicago Press.

Przeworski, Adam, et al. 2000. *Democracy and Development: Political Institutions and Material Well-Being in the World. 1950–1990*. Cambridge: Cambridge University Press.

Putnam, Robert D. 1993. *Making Democracy Work: Civic Traditions in Modern Italy*. Princeton, NJ: Princeton University Press.

Radaelli, Claudio, and Vivien Schmidt, eds. 2005. *Policy Change and Discourse in Europe*. London: Routledge.

Robb, Alan, and Susan Newberry. 2007. "Globalization: Governmental Accounting and International Financial Reporting Standards." *Socio-Economic Review* 5: 725–54.

Roe, Mark. 2006. *Political Determinants of Corporate Governance: Political Context, Corporate Impact*. Oxford: Oxford University Press.

Ross, George. 1995. *Jacque Delors and European Integration*. New York: Oxford University Press.

Rousseau, Denise M. 1989. "Psychological and Implied Contracts in Organizations." *Employee Responsibilities and Rights Journal* 2: 121–39.

Roy, William G. 1997. *Socializing Capital: The Rise of the Large Industrial Corporation in America*. Princeton, NJ: Princeton University Press.

Sack, Kevin. 2008. "Illegal Farm Workers Resort to Health Care in the Shadows." *New York Times*, May 10.

Sáez, Lawrence, and Julia Gallagher. 2009. "Authoritarianism and Development in the Third World." *Brown Journal of World Affairs* 15: 87–101.

Sahlin-Andersson, Kerstin. 1996. "Imitating by Editing Success: The Construction of Organization Fields." In *Translating Organizational Change*. Czarniawska, Barbara, and Guje Sevón, eds. New York: Walter de Gruyter, pp. 69–92.

Sapat, Alka. 2004. "Devolution and Innovation: The Adoption of State Environmental Policy Innovations by Administrative Agencies." *Public Administration Review* 64: 141–51.

Sassen, Saskia. 1999. "Making the Global Economy Run: The Role of National States and Private Agents." *International Social Science Journal* 51: 409–16.

Sauder, Michael, and Gary Alan Fine. 2008. "Arbiters, Entrepreneurs, and the Shaping of Business School Reputations." *Sociological Forum* 23: 699–723.

Schmidt, Vivien, A. 2001. "The Politics of Economic Adjustment in France and Britain: When Does Discourse Matter?" *Journal of European Public Policy* 8: 247–64.

References

Schneiberg, Marc. 2007. "What's on the Path? Path Dependence, Organizational Diversity and the Problem of Institutional Change in the US Economy, 1900–1950." *Socio-Economic Review* 5: 47–80.

Schneiberg, Marc, and Tim Bartley. 2001. "Regulating American Industries: Markets, Politics and the Institutional Determinants of Fire Insurance Regulation." *American Journal of Sociology* 107: 101–46.

Schotter, Andrew. 1981. *The Economic Theory of Social Institutions*. Cambridge: Cambridge University Press.

Schultz, Howard, and Dori Jones Yang. 1997. *Pour Your Heart into It: How Starbucks Built a Company One Cup at a Time*. New York: Hyperion.

Scott, Marvin B., and Stanford M. Lyman. 1968. "Accounts." *American Sociological Review* 33: 46–62.

Scott, W. Richard. 1983. "Introduction: From Technology to Environment." In *Organizational Environments: Ritual and Rationality*. Meyer, John W., and W. Richard Scott, eds. Beverly Hills, CA: Sage Publications, pp. 13–17.

Scott, W. Richard. 2001. *Institutions and Organizations*. Thousand Oaks, CA: Sage Publications.

Scott, W. Richard. 2008a. *Institutions and Organizations: Ideas and Interests*. Thousand Oaks, California: Sage Publications.

Scott, W. Richard. 2008b. "Approaching Adulthood: The Maturing of Institutional Theory." *Theory and Society* 37: 427–42.

Sil, Rudra. 2003. "Globalization, the State and Industrial Relations: Common Challenges, Divergent Transitions." In *The Nation-State Under Challenge*. Paul, T. V., et al., eds. Princeton, NJ: Princeton University Press, pp. 260–88.

Simmons, Beth, and Lisa Martin. 2002. "International Organizations and Institutions." In *Handbook of International Relations*. Carlsnaes, Walter, et al., eds. London: Sage Publications, pp. 192–211.

Skocpol, Theda, ed. 1984. *Visions and Methods in Historical Sociology*. New York: Cambridge University Press.

Skocpol, Theda. 1985. "Bringing the State Back in: Strategy of Analysis in Current Research." In *Bringing the State Back In*. Evans, Peter B., et al., eds. Cambridge: Cambridge University Press, pp. 3–35.

Skocpol, Theda. 1995. "Why I Am an Historical Institutionalist." *Polity* 28: 103–6.

Smelser, Neil J., and Richard Swedberg, eds. 2005. *Handbook of Economic Sociology*. Princeton, NJ: Princeton University Press.

Smith, Adam. 2000. *An Inquiry into the Nature and Causes of the Wealth of Nations*. New York: Modern Library.

Song, Eun Young. 2008. "Competing Values in World Culture and the Emergence of Middle Ground." *Comparative Sociology* 7: 28–50.

Spillman, Lyn. 1999. "Enriching Exchange: Cultural Dimensions of Markets." *American Journal of Economics & Sociology* 58: 1047–71.

References

Stark, David. 1986. "Rethinking Internal Labor Markets: New Insights from a Comparative Perspective." *American Sociological Review* 51: 492–504.

Stark, David. 1996. "Recombinant Property in Eastern European Capitalism." *American Journal of Sociology* 101: 993–1027.

Steinmo, Sven. 1993. *Taxation & Democracy: Swedish, British, and American Approaches to Financing the Modern State.* New Haven, CT: Yale University Press.

Stigler, George J. 1961. "The Economics of Information." *The Journal of Political Economy* 69: 213–25.

Stigler, George J. 1971. "The Theory of Economic Regulation." *Bell Journal of Economics* 2: 3–21.

Strang, David, and John W. Meyer. 1994. "Institutional Conditions for Diffusion." In *Institutional Environments and Organizations: Structural Complexity and Individualism.* Scott, W. Richard, and John W. Meyer, eds. Thousand Oaks, CA: Sage Publications, pp. 100–11.

Strang, David, and Mary C. Still. 2004. "In Search of the Elite: Revising a Model of Adaptive Emulation with Evidence from Benchmarking Teams." *Industrial and Corporate Change* 13: 309–33.

Streeck, Wolfgang. 1999. "Beneficial Constraints: On the Economic Limits of Rational Volunteerism." In *Contemporary Capitalism: The Embeddedness of Institutions.* Hollingsworth, J. Rogers, and Robert Boyer, eds. Cambridge: Cambridge University Press, pp. 197–219.

Stryker, Robin. 2003. "Mind the Gap: Law, Institutional Analysis and Socioeconomics." *Socio-Economic Review* 1: 335–67.

Sutton, John R., et al. 1994. "The Legalization of the Workplace." *American Journal of Sociology* 99: 944–71.

Swank, Duane. 2003. "Withering Welfare? Globalization, Political Economic Institutions, and the Foundations of Contemporary Welfare States." In *States and Global Markets: Bringing Domestic Institutions Back in.* Weiss, Linda, ed. Cambridge: Cambridge University Press, pp. 58–83.

Swedberg, Richard, and Mark Granovetter. 2001. "Introduction to the Second Edition." In *The Sociology of Economic Life.* Granovetter, Mark, and Richard Swedberg, eds. Boulder, CO: Westview Press, pp. 1–28.

Tamm Hallström, Kristina. 2004. *Organizing International Standardization: ISO and the IASC in Quest of Authority.* Massachusetts: Edward Elgar Publishing, Inc.

Tate, Jay. 2001. "National Varieties of Standardization." In *Varieties of Capitalism: The Institutional Foundations of Comparative Advantage.* Hall, Peter A., and David Soskice, eds. New York: Oxford University Press, pp. 442–73.

Thelen, Kathleen. 1999. "Historical Institutionalism in Comparative Politics." *Annual Review of Political Science* 2: 369–404.

Thornton, Patricia H., and William Ocasio. 1999. "Institutional Logics and the

References

Historical Contingency of Power in Organizations: Executive Succession in the Higher Education Publishing Industry, 1958–1990." *American Journal of Sociology* 105: 801–43.

Vetterlein, Antje. 2007. "Economic Growth, Poverty Reduction, and the Role of Social Policies: The Evolution of the World Bank's Social Development Approach." *Global Governance* 13: 513–33.

Wagenaar, Alexander C., and Tracy L. Toomey. 2000. "Effects of Minimum Drinking Age Laws: Review and Analyses of the Literature from 1960 to 2000." Prepared for the Advisory Council on College Drinking, National Institute on Alcohol Abuse and Alcoholism.

Wahlke, John C., et al. 1962. *The Legislative System: Explorations in Legislative Behaviour*. New York, NY: Wiley.

Weber, Max. 1978. *Economy and Society: An Outline of Interpretative Sociology*. Berkeley, CA: University of California Press.

Weir, Margaret. 1993. *Politics and Jobs: The Boundaries of Employment Policy in the United States*. Princeton, NJ: Princeton University Press.

Werle, Raymund. 2001. "Institutional Aspects of Standardization – Jurisdictional Conflicts and the Choice of Standardization Organizations." *Journal of European Public Policy* 8: 392–410.

Westney, D. Eleanor. 2001. "Japanese Enterprise Faces the Twenty-First Century." In *The Twenty-First-Century Firm: Changing Economic Organization in International Perspective*. DiMaggio, Paul, ed. Princeton, NJ: Princeton University Press, pp. 105–43.

Westphal, James D., and Edward J. Zajac. 2001. "Decoupling Policy from Practice: The Case of Stock Repurchase Programs." *Administrative Science Quarterly* 46: 202–28.

Wetterberg, Anna. 2007. "Concept vs. Content: The Institutionalization of Labor Self-Regulation in the Global Apparel Industry." *Conference Papers – American Sociological Association, 2007 Annual Meeting*.

Wheelan, Charles. 2002. *Naked Economics: Undressing the Dismal Science*. New York: W. W. Norton.

Wherry, Frederick. 2004. "International Statistics and Social Structure: The Case of the Human Development Index." *International Review of Sociology* 14: 151–69.

White, Harrison C. 2002. *Markets from Networks: Socioeconomic Models of Production*. Princeton, NJ: Princeton University Press.

Williamson, Oliver E. 1975. *Markets and Hierarchies: A Study in the Economics of Internal Organizations*. New York: Free Press.

Williamson, Oliver E. 1985. *The Economic Institutions of Capitalism*. New York: The Free Press.

Wilson, Woodrow. 1890. *The State: Elements of Historical and Practical Politics*. Boston, MA: Heath Publishers.

Wise, Timothy A. 2009. "Agricultural Dumping Under NAFTA: Estimating

References

the Costs of U.S. Agricultural Policies to Mexican Producers." *Global Development and Environment Institute – Working Paper No. 09–08.*

Wonders, Nancy A., and Raymond Michalowski. 2001. "Bodies, Borders, and Sex Tourism in a Globalized World: A Tale of Two Cities – Amsterdam and Havana." *Social Problems* 48: 545–72.

Woods, Ngaire. 2006. *The Globalizers: The IMF, the World Bank, and Their Borrowers.* Ithaca, NY: Cornell University Press.

Woolsey, Theodore D. 1877. *Political Science or the State: Theoretically and Practically Considered.* New York: Charles Scribner's Sons.

World Bank. 1993. *The East Asian Miracle.* Washington, DC: The World Bank.

World Bank. 2007. *Conditionality in Development Policy Lending.* Washington, DC: The World Bank.

World Trade Organization. 2009. *International Trade Statistics.* Washington, DC: Bernan Press.

Zajac, Edward J., and James D. Westphal. 2004. "The Social Construction of Market Value: Institutionalization and Learning Perspectives on Stock Market Reactions." *American Sociological Review* 69: 433–57.

Zand, Dale E. 1972. "Trust and Managerial Problem Solving." *Administrative Science Quarterly* 17: 229–39.

Zelizer, Vivana A. 1978. "Human Values and the Market: The Case of Life Insurance and Death in 19th Century America." *American Journal of Sociology* 84: 591–610.

Zelizer, Viviana A. 1996a. "Payments and Social Ties." *Sociological Forum* 11: 481–95.

Zelizer, Viviana A. 1996b. *Pricing the Priceless Child: The Changing Social Value of Children.* Princeton, NJ: Princeton University Press.

Zelizer, Viviana A. 2005. *The Purchase of Intimacy.* Princeton, NJ: Princeton University Press.

Zhao, Wei. 2009. "Market Institutions, Product Identities, and Valuation of California Premium Wines." *Sociological Quarterly* 50: 525–55.

Zucker, Lynne G. 1986. "Production of Trust: Institutional Sources of Economic Structure, 1840–1920." *Research in Organizational Behavior* 8: 53–111.

Index

Page numbers in bold refer to tables; page numbers in italics refer to figures.

Index

Chile
  economic growth 94, 99, 112
  transition to neoliberal economy
    122–3
China
  authoritarian regimes 113–14
  clean-technology products and
    services 56, 103
  company law 69
  economic growth 94, 99, 112,
    113
  nominal GDP **100**
civil law 151–2
CMEs (Coordinated Market
  Economies) 107–9
coercive institutional mechanisms
  88–9, 93
  see also isomorphism
coffee products 26, 32–4
Cold War 50, 67, 120
Collective Redundancies Directive *see*
  CRD
COMESA **127**, 149, 152, 178
common law 151–2
Commons, John R. 11
conditionalities **135**, 136–7, 142
constructivism 3
Coordinated Market Economies *see*
  CMEs
Corn products 130–1
corporate governance **64**, 67, 69–70,
  93, 175
corporate social responsibility 69,
  71–2
CRD (Collective Redundancies
  Directive) 68

decoupling 20, 92
definitional notions 147–50, 151
democracy **100**
  see also democratic systems of
    governance
democratic systems of governance 96,
  99–102, 113
Denmark 40, 103, 104, 109, **126**
dependency theory 98–9
deregulation 117, 123, 171

developing countries
  grants from the World Bank 142
  informal economies within 173
  labor rights 124
Durkheim, Émile 18, 20

eBay 28, 31, 45
economic identity
  definition of **32**
  established prior to transaction
    51–3
  established through the course of
    transaction 53
  exclusionary practices 54–5
economic output of nations 106–11
economy, definition of 5
efficiency 6, 8, 20, 49, 62, 78, 87,
  93
EFTA **127**, 150, 152
enable, definition of 5
environment, protection of 66, 67, 89,
  129, 148
EU (European Union)
  adoption of legislation 119, 157
  anti-trust legislation 119–20
  ARD 68
  civil law traditions 152–3
  CRD 68
  goodness of fit 128–30
  marketplace 35
  members and objectives **126**
  reduction of barriers to trade 161
  standardization 148–9
  welfare policies
  see also specific countries
Europe 65, 69, 91, 103, 135, 144
  see also specific countries
Europe, Eastern 65, 119, 120
  see also specific countries
European Commission 119, 172
European Union *see* EU
everyday behavior in organizations
  83–6

FDI (Foreign Direct Investment)
  101–2, 121, 124
filtering institutions **65**, 80–3

202

Index

Index

Index

NIE (New Institutional Economics)
  13–14, 17
non-tariff barriers to trade 126, 139,
  140, 161
normative institutional mechanisms
  88, 90, 93
  see also isomorphism
normative notions 147–50
North America 120, 135
  see also specific countries
North American Free Trade
  Agreement *see* NAFTA
North, Douglass 13
  see also Robert Paul Thomas

OMC (Open Method of
  Coordination) 172
Open Method of Coordination *see*
  OMC
organizational field(s) 62, 77
organizational institutionalism 19, 21
organizations
  definition of economic behavior of
    62
  institutions inside of 63, 79–88
  institutions outside of 62, 65–79

Pareto-optimal spaces 17
parties in the exchange 51–5
path dependence 17, **97**, 118, 119
personal retirement 59–60
phenomenology 3
physical location of firms and offices
  75–6
Poland **100**, 118, 119, **126**
power dynamics 7, 85, 104, 110,
  173
predictability 12, 47, 64, 98
preference formation **32**, 55–60
private property 11, 49, 118
privatization 96, 118, 122, 123
product advertising 36
product attributes 32–6
property rights
  definition of **32**
  national output 96
  nature and evolution of 13

poverty 105
  and private property 49–50
prostitution 37, 57, 173

Radical Product Innovation *see* RPI
rankings of colleges and universities
  see UNSWR
rational choice theory 15–16, 153
redistribution of wealth 116, 118
Regional Trade Agreements *see* RTAs
Rover 68
RPI (Radical Product Innovation) 74
RTAs (Regional Trade Agreements)
  creation of regulatory systems
    150–2; standardization approach
    150–1, *see also* civil law; mixed
    approach 150, 152; mutual
    recognition approach 150–1, *see
    also* common law
  definition of **135**
  dominant national traditions and
    the design of **152**
  impact on national economies
    125–31
  institutions of 146–50
  major RTAs in the world **126**
Russia 65, **100**, 118, 119

SAPs (Structural Adjustment
  Programs) 136, 137
Schotter, Andrew 13, 14
shape, definition of 5
Singapore 99, 113, 114, **126**
socialism, transition to capitalism 96,
  118–20
SOEs (State-Owned Enterprises) 9,
  119, 122
soft law **135**, 161, 172, 173, 179
SOPs (Standard Operating
  Procedures) 122
SOs (Standardization Organizations)
  150, 155, 156, 157, 159
South Korea
  authoritarian regimes 114
  chaebols 114
  economic growth 94, 112
  nominal GDP **100**